Children & Libraries

Getting It Right

VIRGINIA A. WALTER

AMERICAN LIBRARY ASSOCIATION
Chicago and London
2001

While extensive effort has gone into ensuring the reliability of information appearing in this book, the publisher makes no warranty, express or implied, as to the accuracy or reliability of the information, and does not assume and hereby disclaims any liability to any person for any loss or damage caused by errors or omissions in this publication.

Cover and text design: Dianne M. Rooney

Composition by ALA Editions in Caxton and Kabel using QuarkXpress 4.1 for a Macintosh

Printed on 50-pound white offset, a pH-neutral stock, and bound in 10-point coated cover stock by McNaughton & Gunn

The paper used in this publication meets the minimum requirements of American National Standard for Information Sciences—Permanence of Paper for Printed Library Materials, ANSI Z39.48-1992. ∞

Library of Congress Cataloging-in-Publication Data

Walter, Virginia A.
   Children and libraries : getting it right / Virginia A. Walter.
      p. cm.
   Includes bibliographical references (p.) and index.
   ISBN 0-8389-0795-4
     1. Children's libraries—United States. 2. Young adults' libraries—United States.
   3. Public libraries—United States. 4. Children's librarians—United States. 5. Young adult services librarians—United States. I. Title.

   Z718.2.U6 W35 2000
   027.62'5—dc21   00-057600

Printed in the United States of America.

05   04   03   02   01   5   4   3   2   1

Contents

Introduction

I SPENT THE LAST SIX MONTHS of the twentieth century writing this book. It was an interesting time for someone to be thinking about the fragile connections between children and libraries in our country.

During the second week in August, a man who had been active in white supremacist activities shot several children in a Jewish community center in Los Angeles. He said he wanted to give America a wakeup call to kill Jews. Earlier in the summer, a man drove his car into a southern California day care center where his ex-girlfriend used to work, killing two children. And the families in Littleton, Colorado, got ready for a new school year. The library at the Columbine High School, where two teenagers had turned their guns on their classmates the previous spring, was hidden from view by a new wall of blue lockers.

The House of Representatives attached a rider to a juvenile justice bill that would require that libraries receiving the special e-rate for telecommunications purposes use filtering software.

In conferences and on electronic discussion lists, librarians debated about the reported inaccuracies of a historical novel about a girl in an Indian boarding school and the ethics of buying the British edition of the popular Harry Potter books in order to put them into the hands of their rabid young American fans before the American edition was published.

Young children were obsessed with Pokemon, playing the Nintendo games and collecting and trading the cards that featured the cute little Japanese cartoon "pocket monsters."

On Thanksgiving Day, a six-year-old boy named Elian Gonzalez was plucked from the ocean sixty miles off of Florida. His mother had embarked from Cuba with a small group of refugees in a rickety boat that tore apart in the rough seas. Only Elian and one other woman survived. The best interests of this little boy would become submerged in a battle between the estranged

Cuban and American sides of his family as he was held up as a symbol of resistance for political activists in both Cuba and the United States.

The Kansas Board of Education voted to discourage the teaching of evolution in the state's classrooms and eliminated the Big Bang from the science curriculum altogether, on the grounds that these two phenomena are only theories.

Closer to home, my grandchildren continued on their separate paths toward literacy. Eight-year-old Vivian was racing through the Harry Potter books along with most of the rest of the kids in this country who read for pleasure. Four-year-old Nadia had learned to "read" David Shannon's "No, David!" (1998) after dozens of repeated readings by her mother, her father, her sister, her grandmother, and anybody else she could cajole. Baby Natasha started her subscription to *Baby Bug* and showed a marked preference for the picture of the butterfly in Tana Hoban's *Black on White* (1993).

As I sit at my computer at home, I can see photos of those three much-loved little girls, the treasures of my heart, as well as a picture I cut from a *Smithsonian* magazine that shows two itinerant musicians, a father and son, sitting by a country road in India, dressed in radiant shades of orange and gold. They are both beaming with pleasure as the man teaches the small boy how to play the beautiful stringed instrument that will be his one day. I keep this picture to remind me of the pleasure of intergenerational connections and to remind me of my responsibility to all children, not just those I know and love. Suzanne Morse (1998), the executive director of the Pew Partnership for Civic Change, tells about a greeting used by Masai warriors in Africa: "How are the children?" The traditional response is, "All the children are well."

My first and strongest motivation in writing this book is my conviction that all the children are not well. I am heartsick at the violence that pervades this country and the terrible harm it is doing to all our children. I am angry that children go homeless and hungry and without adequate medical care in the richest country in the world. I worry about the children who are growing up without basic literacy skills and those who are growing up without exposure to books and ideas that will nourish them and give them dreams. I worry about the children who spend too many hours in front of computer and television screens, and I worry about the children who never have the chance to use a computer at all.

I am convinced that as a nation we are failing our children. I would save them all if I could. I would fix the broken schools and families, the juvenile justice system, and the health care system. I would create communities where children were cherished for who they are and what they contribute to the world now, not just for the money they spend, the votes they can generate, or the adults they will someday be.

For now, I am engaged in a more modest mission, but an important one. I want to fix our libraries. They are not all hopelessly broken. Many of them are glorious kid spaces where children are respected and nurtured. But the needs are so great, and our potential is so strong. We can do it better. We can get it right in every community, for every child.

This is not a how-to-do-it book. It is more of a how-to-think-about-it book. I was influenced initially by Walt Crawford and Michael Gorman's *Future Libraries: Dreams, Madness, and Reality* (1995). As Crawford and Gorman reflected on possible future scenarios, they found it helpful to look back to the historical foundations of the library as an institution and librarianship as a profession. One product of their reconsideration of libraries' traditions was the formulation of a new set of laws of library science, based on the classic laws set forth by Ranganathan in 1931. Here is the new formulation:

> Libraries serve humanity.
>
> Respect all forms by which knowledge is communicated.
>
> Use technology intelligently to enhance service.
>
> Protect free access to knowledge.
>
> Honor the past and create the future (Crawford and Gorman 1995, 8).

Like Crawford and Gorman, I have found it useful to look at the past in order to speculate about the future. In the early days of the American Library Association, the conference proceedings were published nearly verbatim. I could almost hear the voices of the women who spoke with such eloquence about tenement children whose squalid lives would be enriched through reading, about the rural children who needed better access to books, and about the new specialists in children's library services who were working to meet those needs.

In this book, I have tried to honor that past while I think about creating the future. Chapter 1 is a descriptive and evaluative look at the history of library services to children in the United States. Chapter 2 assesses the current status of children's library services. Chapter 3 looks at some warning signs and trouble spots in contemporary library service to children. Chapter 4 examines the ways in which children's lives are changing, creating new opportunities and challenges for the librarians who serve them. Chapter 5 looks at emerging trends in library services that indicate positive responses to changes in children's lives. Chapter 6 presents three alternative visions for library services for children in the twenty-first century. These visions are based on three different conceptualizations of the child of the future: the child as reader, the child of the Information Age, and the child in the community. Librarians will need to think carefully about whether these images of the child are mutually exclusive or whether they can coexist. They will need to design services that meet the needs and circumstances of the children who live in the here and now of the twenty-first century. Chapter 7 offers ten steps for achieving effective library services for future kids, strategies and visions that will help us to get it right. The afterword outlines five laws of children's librarianship to guide us through the next century.

CHAPTER
1

Where We Came From
The Tradition of Public Library Service to Children

WHEN PHILANTHROPISTS AND CIVIC LEADERS established the first public libraries in the United States in the early 1800s, their intentions were to provide good reading to adults who were not wealthy enough to purchase their own books and to help assimilate immigrants from Europe into American society. With very few exceptions, these early libraries were not open to children.

The Beginnings

In 1876, the U.S. Bureau of Education commissioned a study of the "history, condition, and management" of public libraries. In his chapter on public libraries and the young, William I. Fletcher argued forcibly that libraries should change their policies that limited access to children. He based his argument on the need to develop good reading habits and refined reading early in life. He wrote: "If there is any truth in the idea that the public library is not merely a storehouse for the supply of the wants of the reading public, but also and especially an educational institution which shall create wants where they do not exist, then the library ought to bring its influence to bear on the young as early as possible" (p. 414). He warned that if librarians do not reach children while they are young, they will develop a taste for light reading—dime novels and cheap stories. Libraries, he insisted, should provide children with good books that are "instructive and stimulating to the better nature"

(p. 416). Fletcher's passionate message was consistent with other ideas beginning to circulate at that time about the need to reach children early in their lives in order to influence the kind of adults they would become.

During the last two decades of the nineteenth century, the ideas of some new experts in child studies began to spread to other disciplines. John Dewey's ideas about education and G. Stanley Hall's theories about child psychology were particularly influential. The Child Study Association was established and became a forum for interdisciplinary discussion of children's social, physical, emotional, and educational needs (Wishy 1968, 107). Professionals with a particular concern for children emerged in the fields of education, social work, child psychology, and librarianship. This concern, combined with the optimism and the crusading spirit of reform that permeated that age, gave birth to new hope. If children could be nurtured properly, said the experts of that time, perhaps they would grow up to take their places in a better society (Hawes 1999, 26-27).

Librarians, for their part, were convinced that children who were exposed to fine, uplifting literature would grow up to be fine, uplifted adults. Betsy Hearne describes the work of the pioneers of children's library services as a visionary quest in which the "grail was not just information or even knowledge but the enrichment of experience through whole reading, the kind of reading that engulfs the heart as well as engaging the head and ultimately shapes a lifetime" (Hearne and Jenkins 1999, 538).

Little by little, libraries began to open their doors to children. Perhaps influenced by the principles of the progressive movement, public libraries followed in the path of social welfare and recreation services, the justice system, and public health programs and began to offer specialized services for children (Jenkins 1994). By the end of the nineteenth century, children were welcome in a number of libraries across the country—among them Minneapolis, Minnesota; Hartford, Connecticut; Denver, Colorado; and San Francisco, California. In 1896, the Pratt Institute in Brooklyn and the Providence Public Library in Rhode Island opened buildings that featured children's rooms designed for young library users (Thomas 1990).

Anne Carroll Moore, one of the first librarians to work in the children's room at the Pratt Institute, described it as an attractive space furnished with chairs and tables designed with children's physical comfort in mind. The shelves were filled with beautiful art books that were written for adults because as yet there were few books published especially for children. The children's room was intended to be a welcoming, homelike, familiar place filled with art, flowers, and growing plants as well as books. It was a place where children could be surrounded by objects that would inspire their wonder. Moore wrote, "From the low windows, children and grown people looked out upon a terraced playground down which the children rolled and tumbled in summer and coasted in winter "(1961, 66). She makes it sound like paradise.

Frances Jenkins Olcott, the head of the children's department of the Carnegie Library of Pittsburgh, described the functions of the children's room in her report to the American Library Association meeting in Portland, Oregon, in 1905:

> The ideal children's room has a double function. First, it is the place in which the children are being prepared to use the adult library, and we feel that if our rooms fail to develop intelligent, self-helpful readers, we have failed in our main object. Second, the ideal children's room should *take the place of a child's private library,* and it should, as far as possible, give the child a chance to browse among books of all classes and kinds, in a room beautifully proportioned and decorated, and presided over by a genial and sympathetic woman who has a genuine interest in the personalities and preferences of the boys and girls (1905, 73).

As public libraries began to offer books and services for children, they also began to recognize the need for specialist staff—"the genial and sympathetic women with a genuine interest in the preferences of the boys and girls"—to provide for this new clientele. In 1905, Olcott described the characteristics of the ideal applicant to the training school for children's librarians at the Carnegie Library:

> Sympathy with and respect for children, strength of character, a genial nature, a pleasing personality, an instinct for reading character, adaptability, and last but not least, a strong sense of humor. Her home training and education should have given her a love and knowledge of books, a fund of general information, a quick and accurate mind. These qualities are difficult to find combined in one person (p. 75).

Mary Wright Plummer presumably found the right candidates for the job because she hired children's librarians for the Pratt Institute in Brooklyn as early as 1902; and in 1906, Anne Carroll Moore was chosen to supervise children's services at the New York Public Library. She remained there as superintendent of work with children until she retired in 1941 (Sayers 1972). Other young women were also attracted to this field that allowed them to combine a love of reading with the nurturing of children. In a presentation at the annual conference of the American Library Association in 1913, Arthur Bostwick commended children's work as the first specialization within the profession of librarianship and urged that even more specialized training for children's librarians be provided (Volume of children's work, 287-89). Pratt Institute had begun offering lectures on children's library work in 1896, and the Carnegie Library in Pittsburgh offered a training class for children's librarians in 1900. This class developed into a school that trained children's librarians exclusively until 1917, providing a cadre of children's librarians who became early leaders in the field (Fenwick 1976, 341).

Anne Carroll Moore probably did more than anyone in those early years to define and institutionalize public library services for children. By all accounts, she was a remarkable person. If she had been a man in that era when arenas for women's accomplishments were severely limited, she could have made significant contributions in any number of fields. Margaret K. McElderry (1997) reveals that Moore had planned to become a lawyer like her father, but when he died she could not clerk in his office and had to look elsewhere for a career. Fortunately for our field, she found library work instead. Mentored by Mary Wright Plummer and Caroline Hewins, she became an advocate for children early in her library career.

Moore's accomplishments at New York Public Library were extraordinary. She believed that the library should be an inviting, gracious environment for children. As she opened children's rooms in successive branch libraries, she made sure they were attractive and welcoming to young people. She established noncirculating collections of fine children's books to ensure that young library patrons would always be able to read and appreciate great literature in the library. She worked to liberalize circulation policies for young patrons and to expand services to include story hours and cooperative efforts with schools. She developed the children's room at the library's flagship building at Fifth Avenue and 42nd Street into a cultural mecca with an international reputation among writers and illustrators of books for children (Lundin 1998).

Moore believed that the public library could contribute to the socialization of children as well as to their literary development. She instituted a pledge that all children signed when they got their library cards: "When I write my name in this book I promise to take good care of the books I use at home" (Sayers 1972, 68). In this way, children learned their responsibilities as library users and as citizens participating in a civic activity. When I was a children's librarian at the San Francisco Public Library in the early 1960s, one of my tasks was to administer a similar pledge to children before they could receive their library cards. We did not inspect their hands for cleanliness before they could handle the books, however, a practice not unknown in the early days of children's services.

Julie Cummins has observed that Anne Carroll Moore developed her approach to library service to children through exploration of both educational and social service philosophies and practices. She codified her philosophy of children's library services as the "Four Respects," which she communicated to the children's librarians whom she trained. The first was respect for children. Second was respect for children's books. Third was respect for children's librarians as an integral element in the library's organization. Fourth was respect for the professional status of children's librarianship, which Moore herself worked tirelessly to elevate (1999, 27).

Anne Carroll Moore exerted her influence in the publishing community, as well as in the domain of professional librarians. Barbara Bader (1997, 520) notes that Moore and her associates "created the world of children's books as a sodality, a community of interest, and the field of children's literature as a specialty." With her strategic position in New York, she developed personal and professional friendships with editors such as Louise Seaman Bechtel and with children's book authors such as Leslie Brooke, Padraic Colum, Walter de la Mare, and Beatrix Potter. She wrote reviews of children's books for the respected literary journal, *The Bookman*, from 1918 to 1926; and in 1924, she instituted a regular column called "The Three Owls" for the *New York Herald Tribune.* She continued the Three Owls tradition and logo in regular contributions to *Horn Book* from 1936 to 1960 (Vandergrift 1996, 694). Her legacy of sustained criticism of children's literature was an important contribution to the children's book trade, which was developing simultaneously with the growth of children's library services. Writing consistently in the most influential reviewing media of her time, Moore acquired a certain reputation, not always appreciated by people in the publishing world who disagreed with her opinion, as a "taste maker" in the world of children's literature. As Bader points out, her reviews were not intended to be merely guidance for the lay reader; they were also meant to influence the editor, the author, and the entire children's literature community.

Anne Carroll Moore was succeeded by Frances Clarke Sayers at New York Public Library. Sayers was another woman of formidable opinions and abilities. There followed, in libraries throughout the country, a long line of women who brought to children's library services the full measure of their passion, dedication, intelligence, and organizational abilities. A number of scholars (Jenkins 1996; Vandergrift 1996; Lundin 1996) have speculated on the impact that such a strong feminine (and feminist) orientation may have had on our profession. Vandergrift also notes that many of these early leaders in children's librarianship were African American—Augusta Baker, Charlemae Rollins, and Barbara Rollock, to name a few. The overall significance of their contributions has not yet been assessed, but they were certainly responsible for raising awareness about the multiracial nature of the children we serve and the need for more sensitive and less stereotyped books to share with children of all races.

Looking at the canon of influential professional literature contributed by the early young people's librarians and their protégés—Annis Duff, Margaret A. Edwards, Paul Hazard, Bertha E. Mahony, Anne Carroll Moore, Amelia H. Munson, Ruth Sawyer, Frances Clarke Sayers, Marie L. Shedlock, Lillian Smith, and Ruth Hill Viguers—Christine Jenkins finds seven articles of faith that permeate the writings:

1. a belief in the primacy and uniqueness of the individual child
2. a belief in the critical importance of individual choice in young people's reading
3. a firm belief in the strength and resilience of young people
4. a belief in the children's room as an egalitarian republic of readers
5. a belief in literature as a positive force for understanding not only between individuals, but also between groups, and nations
6. a friendly and unsentimental older sister's attitude towards children
7. an assumption that children's librarians would prevail over adversity in the performance of their professional work (Hearne and Jenkins 1999, 552-58)

Although these core beliefs are part of the heritage and ideology of most librarians working with children today, it can be argued that the strength of their conviction has diminished. Few contemporary children's librarians approach their work with the same passion and near-religious fervor the pioneers of our profession exuded. As Jenkins writes, "Invested in both communion and crusade, the foremothers of children's librarianship created a new testament of faith in the miraculous powers of the word" (Hearne and Jenkins 1999, 558).

Expansion and Outreach

Sara Innis Fenwick (1976) points out that from the 1920s until the 1950s libraries across the country began adopting children's library practices that had been developed with such energy and innovation in the early part of the century. During this time of diffusion, children's services became an institutionalized part of public library offerings. Some libraries offered specialized services to young adults during this time, but no other significant changes in the structure or patterns of service for young people occurred until after World War II.

Public library services got a big boost in 1956, when the federal government passed the Library Services Act, later known as the Library Services and Construction Act (LSCA). The act funded both construction and demonstration projects. The additional money that trickled down to local communities under this legislation enabled many libraries to expand their basic services and to experiment with new kinds of programs. Libraries were also eligible for some of the War on Poverty programs of the Johnson administration. There was an impetus to reach new populations, to "serve the unserved," and outreach became a new buzzword in the profession (Molz and Dain 1999).

During the 1960s, outreach programs were designed to take library programs outside the walls of the library to nonwhite and economically disadvantaged people who were not traditional library users. Libraries experimented with new kinds of mobile services. Outreach librarians also tried to attract new users with innovative programs ranging from tricycle races in the parking lot to African dance presentations. Children were the most frequent outreach targets. Children's librarians told stories to groups of kids in housing project playgrounds and at street festivals. Many libraries' book collections blossomed with more multicultural content than they ever had before (Fenwick 1976, 355-56). Unfortunately, the impact of the era of big federal aid on services to children has not been measured (Willett 1995, 94ff.). Although many programs were abandoned when federal aid was withdrawn, outreach and community cooperation became established during this period as good practice for children's library services and continue in many libraries to this day.

The latest enactment of federal legislation for libraries is the Library Services and Technology Act (LSTA), authorized for the first time in 1997. As the name implies, its focus is on technology. In addition to funding the development of electronic information resources and the establishment of electronic linkages among libraries and other service providers, however, it also aims to improve the provision of library services to underserved populations. LSTA funds are allocated as follows: 91.5 percent to state library agencies that distribute them to libraries in their jurisdictions for a variety of purposes; 4 percent to competitive national leadership grants that provide for education and training of library personnel, research and demonstration projects, preservation and digitization projects, and model cooperative activities between libraries and museums; and 1.5 percent to services for Indian tribes. These programs are all administered by a new agency, the Institute of Museum and Library Services (IMLS).

The Library Services and Technology Act takes federal responsibility for public library services out of the U.S. Department of Education, where it has been located for more than a hundred years (Molz and Dain 1999, 104ff.). It is still too early to know what impact the changes represented by LSTA and IMLS will have on library services to children, but children's library services do not appear to be an initial priority. Out of the forty-two programs that received national leadership grants in 1998, only three are specifically geared to children. The primary grantee on each of those programs is a museum, with a library named as a community partner. Some of the other programs, such as the initiative to recruit diverse students to the master's degree program in library science at the University of Maryland and the project based at the St. Louis Public Library to refine a case-study methodology for determining the economic benefits of services offered by large public libraries, may benefit children's services as well, but that is not their primary objective.

The Era of Accountability

During the 1980s, local governments throughout the country experienced budgetary shortfalls caused by regional economic downturns and changes in tax structures such as Proposition 13 in California. One of the responses was a renewed emphasis on documenting productivity and accountability for results in government agencies, including libraries. The authors of an influential book from this period, *Reinventing Government: How the Entrepreneurial Spirit Is Transforming the Public Sector*, pointed out a significant governmental shift from funding inputs to funding outputs (Osborne and Gaebler 1992). Policy makers were demanding to know what kind of return they would get from their increasingly limited financial investment.

Accordingly, department managers were being asked to anticipate results in their budget requests and to provide quantifiable measures of their achievements. Many library managers were forced to look beyond their traditional circulation and reference use counts for more descriptive and reliable ways to account for their outputs.

The Public Library Association (PLA), a division of the American Library Association (ALA), responded to this need for more comprehensive measurement techniques with *Output Measures for Public Libraries,* second edition (Van House et al. 1987), a companion to *Planning and Role Setting for Public Libraries* (McClure et al. 1987). These manuals, intended to be general and comprehensive, did not deal specifically with any elements of library service to children other than those associated with the Preschoolers' Door to Learning. The authors presumed that libraries could adapt the planning process and measurement techniques to any specialized services that were appropriate for their organizations.

Adele Fasick (1990) has observed that children's librarians have often resented and resisted having to evaluate the services they provide. Some have argued that the important services are intangible and unquantifiable: How does one compute the value of good reading in a child's life? Some have felt defensive about having to constantly justify the worth of a service that is typically underfunded and undervalued. Others have been concerned that existing techniques for measuring general library services, such as *Output Measures for Public Libraries*, do not adequately capture the outputs of library services for children. This concern was partially mitigated by the publication of *Output Measures for Public Library Service to Children* (Walter 1992).

Output Measures for Public Library Service to Children is a manual of standardized procedures for collecting, interpreting, and using quantitative data that measure the outputs of children's services. It delineates the following output measures:

Library Use Measures

> *Children's Library Visits per Child* is the average number of visits per child to the library by people age 14 and younger in the community served. It measures walk-in use of the library.

> *Building Use by Children* indicates the average number of people 14 and under who are in the library at any particular time. Together

with Children's Library Visits per Child, this measure shows patterns of use.

Furniture/Equipment Use by Children measures the proportion of time, on average, that a particular type of furniture or equipment, such as preschool seating or computer terminals, is in use by people 14 and under.

Materials Use Measures

Circulation of Children's Materials per Child measures the use of children's library materials loaned for use outside the library, relative to the number of people age 14 and under in the service area.

In-Library Use of Children's Materials per Child indicates the use of children's library materials within the library, relative to the number of people age 14 and under in the community served.

Turnover Rate of Children's Materials indicates the intensity of use of the children's collection, relating the circulation of children's materials to the total size of the children's collection.

Materials Availability Measures

Children's Fill Rate is the percentage of successful searches for library materials by users age 14 and under and adults acting on behalf of children.

Homework Fill Rate is the proportion of successful searches for information or library materials for homework use by library users age 14 and under and adults acting on behalf of children.

Picture Book Fill Rate is the percentage of successful searches for picture books.

Information Services Measures

Children's Information Transactions per Child is the number of information transactions per person age 14 and under in the community served made by library users age 14 and under and by adults acting on behalf of children.

Children's Information Transaction Completion Rate is the percentage of successful information transactions by persons age 14 and under and by adults acting on behalf of children.

Programming Measure

Children's Program Attendance per Child measures annual attendance at children's library programs per person age 14 and under in the community served.

Community Relations

Class Visit Rate measures visits from school classes to the library relative to the total number of school classes in the community.

Child Care Center Contact Rate is the number of contacts between the library and child care centers relative to the number of child care centers in the community.

Annual Number of Community Contacts is the total number of community contacts made by library staff responsible for service to children during the year.

Librarians have used the specialized output measures for children's services and a companion volume, *Output Measures and More: Planning and Evaluating Public Library Services for Young Adults* (Walter 1995), to formulate budget requests, to make informed decisions about service patterns and resource allocations, to evaluate grant-funded projects, to compare youth services to other elements in the overall programming, and to measure progress toward various management objectives. The use of these management information tools represents a shift for many children's librarians toward accountability and a willingness to judge the effectiveness of their work.

The latest iteration of a planning process by the Public Library Association eliminated the Preschoolers' Door to Learning from its menu of service responses. The new list of thirteen service responses is intended to be a more specific representation of public library responses to community needs than the more general library roles had been. The service responses are:

basic literacy	formal learning support
business and career information	general information
commons	government information
community referral	information literacy
consumer information	lifelong learning
cultural awareness	local history and genealogy
current topics and titles	

The authors of the guidebook for this new planning process, *Planning for Results*, observe that none of these roles is age-specific. All of the service responses can be applied to all categories of people in a community. They write, "The Preschoolers' Door to Learning role included in *Planning and Role Setting for Public Libraries* described one important, but narrow, aspect of service to children. Because there was only one age-specific role, services for children and youth were often isolated into that single role in the plans many libraries developed even though that was not the way the original role was conceived" (Himmel and Wilson 1998, 29). Children's librarians will be monitoring the results of this change to be sure that libraries are considering the needs of children as they adopt this new way of planning their overall services.

Increasingly, children's librarians demand to be seen as managers. In many libraries, a children's services coordinator is a member of the administrative team. Even children's librarians who work alone in small library agencies assume management responsibilities as they assess their communities; plan, implement, market, and evaluate programs and services; supervise pages and volunteers; manage complex multimedia collections; raise funds; and network with other youth-serving professionals. Of course, they still tell stories, provide reference and readers' advisory assistance, compile book lists and bibliographies, create bulletin board displays, teach Internet classes to children and parents, and participate in professional associations such as the Association for Library Service to Children. It is a measure of the widespread acceptance of this concept of the children's librarian as a manager that a book published by the American Library Association in 1995, *Youth Services Librarians as Managers* (Staerkel et al.), included chapters on planning, budgeting, grantsmanship, policies and procedures, evaluation, personnel issues, recruitment, strategies for conducting effective meetings, and networking and cooperation. Although the context for these topics was library service to children, the topics themselves are suited to a general management textbook.

The Legacy

As I examine our historical record, I see three enduring elements, one from each of the periods examined above, that still affect how children's librarians think about themselves and their clientele and how they deliver library services today.

Perhaps the strongest legacy from the rich historical roots of children's library services is a concept of the child as reader. From the very beginning, those who were most passionate about library services to children were also passionate about the presumed benefits of reading fine books during childhood. Great attention has been given, therefore, to identifying the best books for children and to developing effective ways for sharing literature with children. More recently, children's librarians have accepted the fact that not all children are able or even motivated to read fine literature, and the new mission for many professionals is simply to get kids to read, period. Nevertheless, it is the child as reader—or potential reader—to whom children's librarians provide their services. Even storytelling programs for preschool children are characterized as preliteracy activities (Jeffery 1995; Nespecca 1994). When they look at the inhabitants of their domains, schoolteachers see students; social workers see dependent members of a family structure; soccer coaches see young athletes; pediatricians see healthy children and sick children; police officers see good children and bad ones; marketing experts see customers. Children's librarians see readers.

The second part of the legacy is a tradition of outreach to the unserved or the underserved. Not only are children's librarians people with a mission; they are also missionaries, eager to spread the word and win converts. At the beginning of the twentieth century, children's librarians strategized about how to deliver services to children working in sweatshops, isolated in rural areas, or living in urban tenements with immigrant parents. Now they look for innovative ways to reach youth who are at risk of not reaching their full potential for a variety of reasons. They enter into collaborative partnerships with agencies and organizations as diverse as low-income health clinics, senior citizen groups, and day care centers in order to extend the library's services into the community.

The outreach tradition has been extended today to a more general commitment to advocacy for children. Children's librarians are joining with other child-serving professionals in networks that lobby for increased awareness of children's needs and more funding for children's programs. Children's librarians also see themselves as advocates within their own libraries and professional associations. They are ready to speak and act for children's interests, much as William I. Fletcher did more than one hundred years ago. There is a new impetus to be represented at the decision-making tables. The outreach tradition and the focus on advocacy have led to the need for more sophisticated political skills.

In 1990, Virginia H. Mathews, Judith G. Flum, and Karen A. Whitney worked on behalf of the three youth-serving divisions of ALA (American Association of School Librarians, Association for Library Service to Children, and Young Adult Library Services Association) to prepare a position paper for the second White House Conference on Library and Information Services. It is a model advocacy document, spelling out needs that are unmet for most American children and demonstrating how libraries can help to meet those needs. A brief statement about the sorry state of funding for library service to youth is followed by proposals for immediate action. The careful preparation of this document and skilled lobbying by its proponents persuaded conference participants to adopt an Omnibus Children and Youth Literacy through Libraries Initiative as a priority in July 1991 (Kids need libraries 1997). Although the library community was less successful in getting legislation passed to advance the initiative, getting youth services to the top of a major national policy agenda was a stunning accomplishment for the librarians who spearheaded this advocacy campaign.

The third portion of our inheritance is a renewed commitment to accountability and managerial excellence. Some children's librarians have formal managerial responsibilities that are recognized by a job title such as children's services coordinator and an appropriate position in the library's organization chart. All children's librarians, however, even those providing frontline service in a small branch library, are managing an important element in their organization's overall operation. The children's librarian manages a collection; plans, implements, and evaluates programs such as summer reading clubs and toddler story times; markets her services in a variety of ways; maintains good working relationships with other child-serving professionals in her community; and coordinates activities for children with other library staff. She often supervises clerical staff and volunteers. Increasingly, children's librarians see themselves as managers as well as professionals. They embrace managerial strategies borrowed from the private sector and from public administration in their efforts to translate good intentions into reality.

Diversity is an issue in our field in the twenty-first century. Children's librarianship is still an overwhelmingly female profession, for example, (whether it is a feminist profession is less clear), although men do make valuable contributions as frontline children's librarians, as managers, and as leaders in professional associations. And, like the rest of the profession, children's librarians are overwhelmingly white, although there is little doubt that the diverse, multicultural children libraries hope to reach would be better served by more diverse, multicultural children's librarians.

Children's librarians have long seen themselves as undervalued within the larger profession. Twenty years ago, Pauline Wilson wrote about a perceived denigration of children's services throughout the country. Much as I will be doing in this book, she summarized the social changes that were affecting children, their reading, and their library use at that time. Then she issued several challenges to children's librarians that bear repeating more than twenty years later. She urged the profession to clarify the role of children's librarians and their relationship to children's literature. Do children's librarians serve children or children's literature? She challenged children's librarians to specify how they enhance the development of a child and to present this evidence clearly and without sentimentality. She warned children's librarians to be aware of the undesirable impression they sometimes convey to their colleagues as people who talk only about children's books and care little about other aspects of library service. She talked about the need to define the competencies of a children's librarian and to determine the kind of education that would best prepare someone for that specialization.

Has progress been made during the last twenty years? Yes and no. Beginning children's librarians are still paid less on average than other public service librarians, according to the 1997 Placements and Salaries Survey (Gregory and McCook 1998). Like all undervalued workers, they often sound disgruntled when speaking among themselves on electronic discussion lists and in conference sessions. Yet their public rhetoric is usually upbeat and optimistic, and they advocate for their young clientele. Children's librarians recognize that what they do is important, even if other people do not understand. Both professionals and library educators continue to struggle with a formula that will prepare children's librarians to do the best job possible in rapidly changing times. To that end, the Association for Library Service to Children has developed competencies for children's librarians that are updated in response to changes in the field (see appendix A).

The next chapter will look at what is happening today in public library service to children in the United States, focusing on what libraries do well.

CHAPTER 2

Where We Are Today
Contemporary Public Library Service to Children

THANKS TO THE VISION OF OUR FOREMOTHERS and the ongoing work of many dedicated children's librarians and their supporters, public library service to children is now well established in communities large and small across the country. It is an ongoing success story. In their recent book about the current condition and future direction of the American public library, Redmond Kathleen Molz and Phyllis Dain point out that service to children remains one of the exemplary aspects of this institution, a key component in the overall offerings of libraries everywhere in the United States (1999, 199ff.). In fact, American adults—whether they are parents or not—have come to value the public library in large part because of the services it provides to children. In a public opinion survey conducted by the Benton Foundation in 1996, "providing reading hours and other programs for children" ranked first on a menu of nine library services. It was rated "very important" by 83 percent of the respondents and "moderately important" by another 12 percent (p. 27). Approval ratings don't get much better than this.

The American public's strong approval of children's services in their libraries is good news. This strong acceptance is probably based on a deep conviction that the public library's mission is first and foremost an educational one. Educating children is one of the few broad social functions that most Americans believe the government should provide.

The polls don't reveal what children think about their public libraries, but they do indicate that children are among the library's most active users. Most recent surveys indicate that about 60 percent of all public library users are under the age of eighteen. A survey conducted by the U.S. Department of

Education, National Center for Education Statistics showed, for example, that 37 percent of all public library users were children eleven years of age and younger, while 23 percent were twelve to eighteen years old (1995). This pattern of usage is particularly interesting in light of the relatively small percentage of the typical library's budget that is devoted to children. Children probably also use libraries differently than adults do. With few exceptions, adults use the materials collections in libraries—the books, magazines, videos, and digital resources. They may use reference services to facilitate their access to those collections. Children, on the other hand, use the materials collections, the reference and readers' advisory services, and a wide array of programs.

What We Do Best

For the most part, what we do best is what we have always done best in public library services for children. Children's rooms and children's sections in public libraries look much the same as they did at the turn of the century, except for contemporary shifts in color preferences or furniture design. We see the same small-size tables and chairs, the same low shelving, the same puppet stages and book displays. Only the computers are new.

The services we provide to children look much the same as well. Certainly what we do best reflects the vision and values of the early pioneers in children's library service. We evaluate children's books and provide collections that are carefully chosen to reflect a particular philosophy about children's reading. Based on their knowledge of those collections, librarians advise children and adults on books that will meet specific reading needs. Almost all public libraries provide summer reading programs designed to motivate children to read during their school vacation. Finally, most public libraries provide some kind of story hour, usually for preschool children. We will look at how these traditional services have evolved to meet changing needs and at emerging services that indicate new directions for public library service to children

Book Selection

When pioneering children's librarians like Anne Carroll Moore began offering library services to children at the turn of the century, there were few books published especially for young people. There were a few classics such *as Little Women*, *Alice's Adventures in Wonderland,* and *Gulliver's Travels*, but most juvenile titles were cheaply produced mass market books and didactic tracts of little literary merit. The first challenge for those early children's librarians was thus to find materials with which to stock the newly designed low shelves of the first library children's rooms. They began by combing the adult collections for materials, often beautifully illustrated art books, that would appeal to children.

By the second decade of the century, New York book publishers had begun to see the potential of a new juvenile market. They hired the first children's book editors and began to develop special lines of children's books. Several scholars have noted the complex personal and professional interrelationship between the early children's book editors and librarians (Jenkins 1996; Vandergrift 1996; Lundin 1996). Children's library services and children's book publishing have developed in parallel. School and public libraries remained the primary markets for children's trade books until recently, when cuts in library materials budgets and an increase in the number of bookstores made the retail market relatively more significant. New electronic retail distribution outlets for books, such as amazon.com, will undoubtedly affect the children's book trade in ways we cannot yet predict.

ANNE CARROLL MOORE

From the beginning, Anne Carroll Moore established the principle that the librarian must know the content and quality of the books she offers to her young patrons. Pointing out that many of her first visitors to the Pratt Institute walked miles to get to the library or pooled their streetcar fares so that one child could select books for his friends, she declared, "It clearly would not do to circulate books of which I had no first-hand knowledge and recent experience" (1961, 66). She was determined not to disappoint the children for whom a visit to the library was so important.

As the number of books published for children increased, Moore began to codify her selection principles. In an early essay, she offered some general principles of book selection. First and foremost was the injunction: "Buy only those books of which you have first-hand knowledge and which are going to mean something to you at the time they are bought. Books should satisfy desires or supply needs" (1961, 156). She went on to list other considerations as well: Is the book well written? It is accurate? Is it original? Is it the best book on the subject at the time? Do the pictures add to the text? Is the type easy to read? What is the quality of the paper and the binding? Many librarians would offer similar principles to explain their selection decisions today.

Moore's emphasis on selection criteria and evaluation standards was also part of a strategy to position children's books as real literature. Christine Jenkins notes that Moore's reviews of children's books in *The Bookman* translated the literary standards that had been formulated by the first children's librarians into descriptive evaluations of children's books. These reviews reflected not only Moore's individual opinion, but a collective opinion based on standards that were held by the profession as a whole (Hearne and Jenkins 1999).

FRANCES CLARKE SAYERS

Anne Carroll Moore and the other pioneers of children's librarianship advocated for quality in children's books. Frances Clarke Sayers, Moore's successor at the New York Public Library, was a particularly articulate, passionate spokeswoman for excellence in children's literature. Themes and phrases from a speech Sayers gave at the 1937 ALA Annual Conference in New York, "Lose Not the Nightingale," became much-quoted watchwords among librarians who found that she expressed their own belief in the power of excellent, imaginative literature for children (Jenkins 1996, 818ff.). In this speech, Sayers referred to Hans Christian Andersen's story "The Nightingale." She compared traditional, imaginative literature to the true nightingale and the realistic, didactic literature growing out of the progressive education movement to the inferior, mechanical nightingale. Sayers was venomous in her criticism of educators who exalted children's firsthand experience over their vicarious experiences from literature and of those who were concerned more with reading level than with content. Speaking as the winds of war were already threatening Europe, she asked her audience:

> Of what are we afraid? Of emotion, of experience? We are very tender, it seems to me, of the young, and tenderness is no preparation for a world half mad and savage. What children need to know is not how dairies and bakeries are run; not the organization of industry, but what spiritual disaster is at work in the world today (1965, 66).

On another occasion, writing for *Publishers Weekly*, Sayers challenged authors who would write for children to remember the child that each of them once was. She urged them to explore their deepest emotions and then to share those feelings with their young readers. In words that still resonate today, she said:

> It is, I know, a terrible discipline to convey it in writing, but if you succeed in producing one small thread of genuine feeling, never doubt that some child will recognize it as his own and take hold of it, like a spider in a web, and by that one thread swing himself free into the world of real values. By that one thread he learns to know the true from the false, the genuine from the manufactured, the sincere from the postured, and so arms himself against a bitter time in which depth of feeling is most greatly needed in a world which makes it increasingly difficult to attain (1965, 115).

In a lecture given recently at UCLA, Newbery medalist Katherine Paterson talked about how Sayers's words to would-be authors for children challenged and inspired her when she was beginning to find her voice as a writer for children. She said she is still summoned by books. She writes stories because she loves reading them, and she has experienced over and over again in her own family the "shattering and gracious encounter of illumination and healing" that books can bring (1996, 13). This profound belief in the power of literature for children explains why children's librarians still place so much emphasis on book selection.

A New Concern for Multicultural Materials

While Frances Clarke Sayers was speaking generally of the need for children to read the best literature that librarians could find for them, some African American librarians were raising the consciousness of the profession and the publishing industry about the images of black children in what Nancy Larrick in 1965 memorably called the "all-white world of children's books." Barbara Rollock observed that up until the 1960s, literature for children featured white, Anglo-Saxon, Protestant characters. Other races, religions, and ethnicities were either absent or depicted with negative stereotypes and slurs (1988, 154). Charlemae Rollins and Augusta Baker suggested guidelines for portrayals of blacks in books early on, but it wasn't until the increased social awareness of the 1960s—and the lure of new markets—filtered into the children's publishing industry that changes were noticeable.

Progress has been slow, but now fine books for children by African American authors and illustrators are found on the lists of most publishing houses; and libraries are buying them, particularly for communities with significant African American populations. In her Ph.D. dissertation, Malore Brown (1996) found that the ethnic composition of a community strongly influences the materials a library selects for it. We must hope that these excellent books by African American authors and illustrators are not being segregated in collections intended primarily for African American readers. All boys and girls should have the opportunity to read these books.

Evaluating multicultural materials has added new dimensions to book selection. These materials must be evaluated not only on the criteria applied to all other children's books—accuracy, literary quality, etc.—but also on their cultural accuracy and authenticity. Not all reviewers feel qualified to make these evaluations, particularly for materials outside of their own culture. Fortunately, there are some excellent guides to help librarians navigate the waters of multiculturalism.

Some children's librarians use the guidelines suggested by the Council on Interracial Books for Children (1980) to analyze materials for sexism and racism. These are reprinted in several widely available sources. Rudine Sims's landmark study, *Shadow and Substance* (1982), pinpoints critical issues about the African American perspective in children's books, while *Through Indian Eyes*, by Beverly Slapin and Doris Seale (1992), has helped many people understand the perspective of Native American people. In addition to print sources such as these, Dana Watson (1998) points to the many guides to selecting and evaluating multicultural children's literature that are available on the World Wide Web. These on-line resources have the advantage of continual updating and references to the most current titles.

An additional impetus to the development of multicultural literature for children has been the establishment of national awards for authors and illustrators of color. The Coretta Scott King Award has been given annually since 1969 by the Social Responsibilities Round Table of the American Library Association to African American authors and illustrators who have made outstanding contributions to literature for children and young adults. In 1996, the Association for Library Service to Children and Reforma established the Pura Belpre Award to honor Latino or Latino writers and illustrators of books for young people. This biennial award is named for the New York Public Library's first Latina librarian. By recognizing distinguished authors and illustrators of color, these awards raise awareness of excellent multicultural literature and may even stimulate new markets for these books. Noted author Virginia Hamilton suggests that in celebrating the thirtieth anniversary of the

Coretta Scott King Award, libraries should build collections of the award-winning books to ensure that children everywhere will be able to read them (1999).

All mainstream children's book publishers now regularly include titles by and about people of color in their offerings. A few smaller publishers are focusing exclusively on multicultural materials. Two effective multicultural publishers are Lee and Low in New York and Children's Book Press in San Francisco. Their books have been named ALA notable books and have won Coretta Scott King and Pura Belpre Awards. The multicultural situation is not as good as it should be, but it is a lot better than it was when Nancy Larrick sounded her warning call in 1965.

From Book Selection to Collection Development

Book selection is now seen as just one aspect of collection development, a broader function that involves selecting, maintaining, and withdrawing materials in a broad range of formats. In collection development, one evaluates books not only for their intrinsic quality, but also for their relationship to other materials in a given collection and their potential use by the library's patrons. Nell Colburn introduced an article on collection development tips with the assertion that an outstanding children's collection is never an accident. "It is the result of careful management, including strategic planning, conscientious budgeting, teamwork, and ongoing evaluation" (1994, 130). Many children's librarians consider collection development to be their most important work.

Much of the library profession's ideology about intellectual freedom rests on a notion of a balanced collection that gives its users the broadest possible points of view on the broadest possible range of topics. There are at least two dimensions of balance in this ideal collection: balance of points of view and balance of subjects covered. This perspective is still represented in the rhetoric of the library profession. It can be seen in the statement, "Libraries: An American Value," adopted by the Council of the American Library Association on February 3, 1999. This document is clearly meant to shore up the association's stand on intellectual freedom in the face of attacks on free access to the Internet, particularly by children. The statement affirms the library's contract with the American people. Its final affirming principle is that of the balanced collection: "We celebrate and preserve our democratic society by making available the widest possible range of viewpoints, opinions and ideas, so that all individuals have the opportunity to become lifelong learners— informed, literate, educated, and culturally enriched."

It has become easier to develop children's collections with broad and balanced subject coverage as publishers have become less cautious about the kinds of books they produce for children. Children's librarians are able to find good nonfiction books on many topics that go beyond the conventional notion of what is appropriate for children. Here are a few examples from recent publishers' lists:

personal safety—*Safe Zone* by Donna Chaiet (1998)

entrepreneurship—*Once upon a Company* by Wendy Halperin (1998)

a Tibetan spiritual leader—*The Dalai Lama* by Demi (1998)

the Holocaust—*Witnesses to War* by Michael Leapman (1998)

AIDS—*HIV Positive* by Bernard Wolf (1997)

Contemporary child slavery in the Third World—*Iqbal Masih and the Crusaders against Child Slavery* by Susan Kuklin (1998)

QUALITY VERSUS POPULARITY

In practice, however, the balanced collection has given way in many public libraries to a market-driven collection. Will Manley (1990) blamed California librarians for adopting this approach after taxpayers passed Proposition 13, slashing property taxes by more than 50 percent and seriously undermining the financial base of public libraries in the state. One response that Manley observed was an abandonment of the traditional balanced collections based on quality. Instead, faced with radically decreased book budgets and the need to woo supporters by any means necessary, librarians adopted the high-volume, low-title approach of chain bookstores and bought the popular materials that patrons demanded. This approach produced happy library customers and high circulation statistics that librarians could use to demonstrate need for continued budget increases.

For children's librarians, the quality versus popularity debate is particularly thorny. The proud tradition of the field is based on nurturing children with the best possible literature. Increasingly, however, the kids don't seem to want to read the best possible literature. They want Goosebumps or the Babysitters Club or whatever the current popular series happens to be. They want the media tie-ins, the books generated by popular movies such as *Star Wars,* and fads such as Pokemon. Barbara Genco (1991) includes these products of children's popular culture in the collections she develops. She reasons that their low price and high appeal make them good bait for reluctant readers. She also defends a child's right to choose the books he or she wants to read, rather than being limited to the materials approved by quality-seeking librarians. For her, the issue is not quality versus popularity, but finding a balance between the two.

Eleanor K. MacDonald on the other hand, takes a firm stand on the side of providing only quality materials for children in a public library. She writes, "The only advantage that mass market materials have over other materials is that they are familiar to children, not more relevant, not easier, just presold" (Genco, MacDonald, and Hearne 1991, 118). She acknowledges that librarians might have to work harder to sell quality books to children because those books don't have the marketing machines behind them that the popular culture books do. In the tradition of Frances Clarke Sayers, MacDonald urges children's librarians to continue offering the "real thing" in spite of the seductive appeal and empty calories of the glittery pop culture products.

In practice, most children's librarians today probably compromise, buying enough of the mass market or current interest titles to keep the children interested and enough of the more enduring titles to keep the faith with their long-standing professional values. Every now and then a librarian reports some unexpected success with a program that piques children's interest in the less accessible literary works in their collections. Roger Kelly, director of the main children's room at the Pasadena Public Library, where popular books mingle with excellent literature on the beautiful wooden shelves, ran a series on the classics for older school-age children as part of his 1999 summer reading program. Focusing on one book each week—*Alice's Adventures in Wonderland, Peter Pan*, Frank L. Baum's Oz books, *Jungle Book, The Second Jungle Book,* and *Charlotte's Web*—he talked about the authors and the times in which the books were written, and he showed clips from movie versions of the stories. It was an experiment, and he was gratified to see the number of participants increase each week. The program appealed to boys as well as girls, and children checked out the books to read for themselves. Parents came, too, and enjoyed learning more about the classics many of them had never read.

CENSORSHIP

Children's librarians are socialized to resist challenges to intellectual freedom just as other librarians do. The Association for Library Service to Children defends children's right to read just as strongly as its parent organization, the

ALA, defends the intellectual freedom of all Americans. Many thoughtful youth services librarians acknowledge, however, that intellectual freedom is a little more complicated when children are involved. At issue is whether children, with their limited life experiences and undeveloped critical thinking skills, are able to make informed judgments about their reading materials. Are they likely to be harmed or negatively influenced in some way by reading material that presents misinformation, negative stereotypes, or explicit sexual content?

In a revealing statement, Barbara Rollock writes, "Good selection practice dictates a degree of objectivity and a high sense of social awareness and sensitivity, but since each selector brings a particular body of experience and subjectivity to the process, there is no absolute neutrality or 'purity' in the process" (1988, 154). She underscores the fine line between selection and censorship. In many situations, children's librarians have found a tension between their objective adherence to intellectual freedom principles and their high sense of social awareness and sensitivity to the children they serve. Should a book be withdrawn from a children's collection because of a racial stereotype, for example? Some of the early Newbery Award winners, honored as the finest contributions to children's literature during their years of publication, are marred by racial stereotypes. Again, Rollock is instructive: "Librarians must weigh whether an image or characterization in a book is only slightly out of balance, but that this fault is outweighed by other good aspects, or whether it has the potential to be actively painful or harmful to the self-image of any group of children or to the perception of them by others" (1988, 155).

In the current climate of political correctness, children's books with non-white characters probably get more scrutiny than other types of books; yet controversies still erupt. The picture book *Nappy Hair* by Carolivia Herron (1997) is an instructive example, although the venue for this controversy was a public school rather than a library. This book, written by an African American woman in a traditional southern black call-and-response format and dialect, was intended to promote ethnic pride. At a family reunion, the grandfather tells the assembled relatives the hyperbolic story of one of the children there, a girl whose hair is unusually kinky. A young white teacher found that her third-grade students, mostly Latino and African American, responded enthusiastically to it. The parents, who learned about the book through the photocopied pages the teacher sent home with the children, were outraged that a white teacher would deal with such a racially sensitive topic, pointing out that "nappy" is still considered a put-down in the African

American community. After a confrontation with the parents that became physically threatening, the teacher resigned (Clemetson 1998; Goldman 1998).

Even more recently, a historical novel by Ann Rinaldi, *My Heart Is on the Ground: The Diary of Nannie Little Rose, a Sioux Girl* (1999), has been charged with errors and misconceptions about Native Americans. Librarians have criticized this book, part of the popular Dear America series from Scholastic, for misidentifying tribal ancestries and failing to address the severity of the suffering of Native American children who were forced to leave their homes and attend government boarding schools ("Native American Fact—or Fiction?" 1999).

However, more challenges seem to come from the conservative, religious right these days than from adults demanding the eradication of racial stereotypes from children's literature. In some communities, parents are asking that books on creationism balance those on evolution. Some folklore is challenged because it is tainted by witchcraft, and some books are criticized as being too frightening for children. Recently, some Christian parents have criticized the wildly popular Harry Potter books by British author J. K. Rowling, featuring the adventures of a young boy being educated at a boarding school for witches and wizards, for their lighthearted approach to witchcraft. Young adult books are sometimes challenged for sexual content or objectionable language.

Among the eight most challenged books recorded by the ALA Office of Intellectual Freedom in 1998 are three children's books: *The Giver* by Lois Lowry (1993), charged with being violent and sexually explicit, using offensive language, and dealing with infanticide and euthanasia; *Crazy Lady!* by Jane Conly (1993), challenged for using offensive language; and *Blubber* by Judy Blume (1983), challenged for using offensive language and being inappropriate for children. The one young adult title on the top eight list, *The Chocolate War* by Robert Cormier (1974), is accused of being sexually explicit. Two juvenile series—Goosebumps and Fear Street—both written by R. L. Stine, have been challenged frequently for being too frightening for children and for depicting occult or satanic themes.

The Challenge of Nonprint Materials

While children's librarians have gloried in their passion for book selection, they have not been as interested in nonprint materials. Most children's collections today include both audio and video materials, but librarians expend much less effort on their selection than they do on book selection. The Association for Library Service to Children lists notable recordings and notable videos and even awards the Carnegie Medal to the most distinguished video for children, but these efforts have not had the impact that similar taste-setting exercises for books have had. In most libraries, the cassettes, compact disks, and videos are add-ons, popular with the patrons but given relatively little attention by the librarians.

Digital materials are creating other issues as well. The first children's software was too unstable and fragile to be circulated to the public, but some libraries made it available on public access computers. CD-ROMs are more durable, and the increasing number of titles with dual-platform formats (Macintosh and Windows) add to their suitability as a circulating item. Children's multimedia software is reviewed in many of the standard library review media, such as *Booklist* and *School Library Journal*; and it is featured in a regular column, "Books and Bytes: Digital Connections," in *Book Links.* I provided guidelines for selecting CD-ROMs for young children in one of those early *Book Links* columns (Walter 1997). It is now common to find educational CD-ROMs available for use on public access computers in children's rooms, and some libraries circulate them with considerable success.

The World Wide Web is more problematic. It resists efforts at control by the most persistent collection development manager. Children's librarians have always selected the books in their collections very carefully, according to the standards in place at their particular library. They were able to justify their selections to anyone who might object or criticize. Now they are faced with a powerful information resource that they cannot control. Even the software filters that block access to words, phrases, or sites considered objectionable do not select or recommend sites that are suitable but only attempt to screen out what is unsuitable.

Most libraries do practice a kind of digital collection development by providing links to useful sites from their home page or by bookmarking sites most likely to appeal to children. If pushed, most children's librarians would agree that their digital resources should be selected with as much care as their print materials. Jane Perlmutter (1999) suggests criteria that might be applied to on-line materials: relevance and use, redundancy, content, ease of use, and stability. The American Library Association (1999) publishes criteria for its 700+ Great Sites: Amazing, Mysterious, Colorful Web Sites for Kids and the Adults Who Care about Them. Ann Symons (1997) offers a twenty-two-point checklist for evaluating Web sites. The San Francisco Public Library (1999) publishes its collection development policy for children's software and Web sites on-line. However, children themselves may not appreciate librarians' efforts to guide them to excellent Web sites. One evaluator for the San Francisco Public Library's Electronic Library Project noted that children preferred the excitement of discovery they got from surfing the Web and finding their own sites to using Web pages that were preselected for them by librarians. He even observed children trading desirable URLs with each other, usually for the game pages and commercial sites considered inappropriate by librarians (Sandvig 1998).

Readers' Advisory and Reference Services

From the beginning, children's librarians have not been content merely to stock their shelves with the best (or most popular) books. They have also actively promoted those books to children and provided specialized one-on-one reading guidance to their young patrons. Anne Carroll Moore's motto, "the right book for the right child at the right time," has inspired librarians to meet the individualized reading needs and interests of every child. Jane Gardner Connor goes so far as to claim that reference and readers' advisory services are the major responsibilities of librarians working with children (1990, 52).

The survey mentioned earlier that was conducted by the U.S. Department of Education's National Center for Education Statistics found that 97 percent of all public libraries offer reference assistance to children, and 75 percent provide readers' advisory services (1995, 16). Children are heavy users of these services. According to the Public Library Data Service's *Statistical Report '97,* the average number of information transactions (reference or readers' advisory queries) reported per child in the legal service area of the library ranged from a high of 2.4 to a low of 1.0 (1997, 168). In other words, on average, children throughout the country made from one to two reference questions in one year. Interestingly, this is higher than the overall average information transactions per capita, which ranged from 1.7 to 0.7 (p. 112). Children evidently ask for more help at the library reference desk than grownups do, a fact that is rarely reflected in library staffing or training.

Nearly all public services librarians working in public libraries today practice the craft of reference, but children's librarians have elevated readers' advisory, or reading guidance, almost to an art form. Much like the hand selling practiced by a few highly skilled bookstore staff, it involves connecting the child with the book. To do this well, librarians must know both the books and the children. This is the added value that professional librarians bring to the task: their intimate knowledge of the books in their collection, their general knowledge of children's developmental stages, their specific knowledge of the child standing in front of them, and their deep belief that books matter, that they are essential, not just "nice."

Highly skilled children's librarians not only possess firsthand knowledge of the books in their collections, knowledge drawn from actually reading those books, but they also see the relationships between books. These relationships are much more subtle than the connections on-line catalogs can provide, linking books with the same key words or broad subject headings. Children's librarians learn to see the relationship, for example, between a book like *The Borrowers* by Mary Norton (1953) and Janet Taylor Lisle's *Afternoon of the Elves* (1989), which both depict elaborately contrived miniature worlds. They understand that a child's love of J. K. Rowling's phenomenally popular *Harry Potter and the Sorcerer's Stone* (1998) may lead that reader to funny school stories such as Betsy Byars's *The Burning Questions of Bingo Brown* (1988) and the poignant *Joey Pigza Swallowed the Key* by Jack Gantos (1998) as well as to the more obvious links in books about wizards and sorcery.

Because children's librarians see these subtle connections and patterns, where the catalog does not, they are able to help the child who says he wants another book as good as *Hatchet* by Gary Paulsen (1987). They learn how to probe gently and find out just what it was about *Hatchet* that captured his heart. Was it the survival theme? That's easy. There are lots of great survival books, from the magic realism of a homeless boy's odyssey in Jerry Spinelli's *Maniac Magee* (1990) to the frightening realism of Uri Orlev's story of an eleven-year-old boy's experiences in the besieged Warsaw ghetto during World War II, *The Island on Bird Street* (1984). Perhaps it was the idea of wilderness survival that appealed to him. Can the children's librarian possibly tempt him to read about a girl who survived on the great Alaskan snowfields? Would he try *Julie of the Wolves* by Jean George (1972)? Is it the plane crash that fascinates the boy? Is it flying that excites him? Maybe this child would enjoy Laurence Yep's *Dragonwings* (1975). This is sensitive, but perhaps it was the parents' divorce that haunts the boy. The children's librarian will listen for clues without prying too deeply and see if a book like *What Hearts* by Bruce Brooks (1992) strikes a chord. Finally, when the child trusts the librarian because she has given him so many books that were just as good as *Hatchet*, he may let her offer a book that she thinks he will like, even if it has little in common with another beloved title, just because it is well written, nourishing, and altogether wonderful.

And so children's librarians practicing the art of readers' advisory make the connections between the book and the child, or the adult acting on behalf of the child. They learn when to push and when to pull back, when to just leave a pile of books on the table for a child to examine with no pressure at all, when to reassure a child that it won't hurt their feelings if he or she doesn't take any of the books they recommended. They learn to know the "regulars" who gobble up books like popcorn and which children are still unsure of their reading skills or unconvinced about the pleasures of literature. They learn which parents worry about violence in children's stories and which ones need to be weaned from some limited understanding of the definition of a "classic." They learn which teachers will take a risk on a controversial new title and which ones cannot be budged from a very literal-minded, objective view of the world and the curriculum.

They learn, too, if they are very good at this, to listen for the silent, "unasked" questions that children sometimes pose. Children don't formulate questions well, and they usually aren't aware of their own deepest and most important information needs (Walter 1995). Sometimes a sensitive librarian can intuit these needs from small clues the children drop like Hansel's pebbles in the deep woods.

If readers' advisory work often tests librarians' knowledge of the fiction and picture book collection, reference work leads them to the information in our nonfiction and reference stacks and, increasingly, to the rich and frustrating world of the Internet. The conventional wisdom is that most children making use of public library reference services today are there for homework purposes (Reichel 1991). This may be true, but there is little research to prove it. A recent pilot study from Maryland investigating library service by children ages eight to fourteen did disclose that almost 90 percent of the reference questions asked there were school related (Blatchford et al. 1998). Interestingly, and perhaps counterintuitively, Melissa Gross (1997) found that only 32 to 43 percent of the circulation transactions in two Southern California school libraries she studies were school related. At any rate, the perception that children's information queries are likely to be school related has driven both collection development practices and reference service approaches in many libraries. Some librarians report that the need for curriculum-related nonfiction is so strong that they must cut back on their budget allocation for fiction that is intended for pleasure reading. On the other hand, some libraries have instituted policies that limit reference assistance for homework queries, reasoning that children will not get the maximum educational value from their assignments if they don't finish them on their own or that homework help is not the public library's responsibility.

Although children's use of public libraries for homework assignments does strain those collections, the Internet has eased some of this pressure. Walter Minkel and Roxanne Hsu Feldman (1999) found that the World Wide Web can be an effective tool for locating resources for homework assignments, particularly those related to current events, science, entertainment, health, sports and recreation, and technology. They warn librarians, however, that children younger than middle school age will have difficulty handling the text-heavy Web sites, complex search tools, and slow response time of Internet resources.

Chapter 5 will discuss an emerging trend that takes a more proactive approach to children and their homework than traditional reference service has provided. For a variety of reasons, some libraries are actually offering homework assistance to students through special collections, digital resources, and aides or tutors.

Summer Reading Programs

In 1998, the DeWitt Wallace-Reader's Digest Fund, in cooperation with the American Library Association, conducted a survey of current practices in serving youth in 1,500 public libraries throughout the country. The results showed that nearly 100 percent of these libraries, from the tiniest to the biggest, in all parts of the country, offered some kind of reading program, defined as book discussions, storytelling, and summer reading programs, targeted to elementary school children (p. 5). I wish the survey had been more specific as to the kinds of reading programs being offered; my hunch is that nearly all are summer reading programs. The aforementioned survey conducted by the U.S. Department of Education's National Center for Education Statistics reported that 95 percent of all libraries offer summer reading programs (1995, 16).

Jill Locke (1992) discovered that public libraries were conducting summer programs and vacation reading clubs for children as early as 1897. Then, as now, the goal was to motivate children to read during those summer months when they were not required to read for school. At the turn of the last century, librarians were convinced that reading good books would contribute not only to the educational accomplishments of children, but also to their moral development.

We are still waiting for the research study that would prove the latter claim, but at least one much-cited study has demonstrated what all classroom teachers have observed— that children in lower grades who don't practice their reading skills over the summer tend to lose them. Barbara Heyns (1978) found that children who read six or more books over the summer increased their vocabulary scores and their general reading levels more than children who did not read at all. New readers, in particular, must keep in practice or their literacy skills wither.

One study in Los Angeles County found that parents see the benefits of a summer reading program to be primarily educational. They were pleased when their children enjoyed the experience, of course, but some enrolled their very reluctant readers in the hope that it would make a difference in both their attitudes and reading skills (Walter and Markey 1997). Having learned from the study that it was parents who made the decision about participating in the summer reading program, librarians in that system changed their marketing strategy. Subsequent promotions have included direct mail to parents and collaborative marketing efforts with the Los Angeles Dodgers and local museums (Barstow and Markey 1997, 31).

With this educational rationale as an underpinning, summer reading programs for children have become a well-established aspect of most public library services, with some kids reporting that they are third and fourth generation summer reading program participants. There are three typical elements to a library summer reading program: theme, reading incentives, and programming. The theme is used as a public relations hook, a unifying thread that ties the program together visually and conceptually. For example, my local library, the Los Angeles Public Library, is currently using as its theme Imagine the Future. The back of the summer reading folder given to each participant invites the children to imagine themselves in 2005, in 2010, and in 2020. Rosanne Cerny, coordinator of children's and young adult services at Queens Borough Public Library, reports that one of the benefits of the statewide approach is political visibility. She finds that legislators can easily understand the concept of library cooperation when New York librarians share the same summer theme and offer the same activities in every legislative district (Barstow and Markey 1997, 32)

Reading incentives are the tangible rewards that are given to children who reach various goals in the reading program. Those goals may be determined by the library or by the individual child. They may represent numbers of books or pages read, the number of minutes spent in reading, library visits, or some other quantitative measure. Most summer reading programs provide some means for children to keep track of their reading, by recording titles, pages, or minutes read. Some require the children to verify their reading through written or oral book reports. The rewards are often small prizes such as stickers, temporary tattoos, pencils, or bookmarks. Other libraries reward participants at the end of the summer with a certificate or an invitation to a celebration of some kind.

Most librarians now prefer to avoid the kind of competitive summer reading program that rewards the children who read the most books. Some librarians find the whole notion of giving external rewards for reading to be contrary to their understanding of good practice. Educator Alfie Kohn's books, *No Contest: The Case against Competition* (1992) and *Punished by Rewards* (1993), have been influential in developing the argument against behaviorist approaches to reading motivation. Kohn cites studies and theories that demonstrate that manipulating behavior through external incentives ultimately fails to achieve learning objectives.

Programming is the third element in the summer reading package. Some libraries see the special summer programming—often provided by professional entertainers—as an end in itself, providing educational or cultural enrichment to the children. Others see it as another way to motivate children to read, leading children from the clown show to the books about circuses, for example. And some libraries used these programs to generate publicity and to draw new users who might not otherwise come in to check out books. At my local branch of the Los Angeles Public Library, the 1999 summer reading club programs, funded by an impressive array of foundations and corporate sponsors, included a magic show, a paper airplane contest, a puppet show, the creation of a library time capsule, an opportunity to design an alien world, an alligator show, and two storytelling programs.

In some communities, the traditional summer reading program has evolved to meet new needs. Year-round schools have produced year-round reading programs. The burgeoning population of preschool library users has stimulated "read to me" programs in which adults can keep track of the books they read to the small children in their care. Some libraries are experimenting with reading programs for older teens and for families.

Information technology is also affecting library summer reading programs. We are beginning to see computer-based summer activities in addition to the traditional reading motivation efforts. The Multnomah County Library integrates its summer reading program into its children's Web site. In the summer of 1999, the medieval theme of ReadQuest featured knights and dragons. Children could register for the program on the ReadQuest Web site and learn more about the activities being held in the system's libraries. They could also participate in an Internet Quest by exploring the Web sites listed at the library's Homework Center site and then answering "quest"ions on-line. The Pasadena Public Library has posted children's book reports on its 1999 Summer Reading Club Web site.

Storytelling

Anne Carroll Moore credits Mary Wright Plummer as the inspiration for the library story hour. After hearing Marie Shedlock tell stories at an afternoon event at Sherry's ballroom in 1902, Plummer invited her to share her art first with the trustees, directors, and teachers at the Pratt Institute and then with the children at a Saturday morning story hour. Anne Carroll Moore, a young librarian at Pratt, was inspired by Marie Shedlock as well and was determined to make storytelling part of the regular service of the New York Public Library when she went to work as the first head of children's services there in 1906 (Sayers 1972, 82ff.).

Moore wrote, "I had been conscious from the first months of my personal work in a children's room of the need for investing reading with dramatic interest and pictorial tradition, if it were to have any real meaning in the daily lives of hundreds of children who were coming to the library—many of them from very sordid homes—with all the freedom of voluntary and familiar association" (1961, 145). Storytelling would be the technique for accomplishing this. She soon hired Anna Cogswell Tyler to develop the art and practice of storytelling at NYPL, and the library story hour was born. Its purpose was to make stories come alive with animated, spirited telling, to share the oral tradition of great folk literature from around the world, and to encourage children to read these stories on their own.

In those early years, librarians targeted older boys and girls as their storytelling audience. Story hours were scheduled after school and on Saturdays. These programs were often held in a room that was separated from the public space of the children's room, and they often included rituals such as the lighting of a story candle to make the experience even more special. Fire laws have caused librarians to abandon the story candle in most locations, and few librarians offer regular story hours for school age children any longer.

Jane Gardner Connor points out in her *Children's Library Services Handbook* that many contemporary school-age children tend to think that story hours are just for little kids and to prefer more sophisticated programs (1990, 70). It has been my experience, however, that when exposed to traditional oral storytelling, even the most media-blitzed ten-year-old responds enthusiastically. There is still magic in the connection between the story, the teller, and the tale; and children whose experiences are overwhelmingly mediated by a computer or television screen seem to thrive on the intimacy of this person-to-person communication. Students who take my storytelling classes and go on to work in libraries find that they can work traditional storytelling into their services in a variety of ways. They tell stories during school visits, as a part of holiday and summer programs, at community fairs and festivals—and once, memorably, as part of a back-to-school promotion hosted by a local department store.

There is probably less storytelling provided for school-age children in libraries than there once was. In the preface to the second edition of *Storytelling Art and Technique,* Augusta Baker and Ellin Green (1987) acknowledge with some sadness that public libraries have decreased the number of story hours for children between the ages of eight and eleven. Their goal was to instill enough confidence in librarians and teachers that they would share stories with children of all ages on a regular basis. We know that story times are conducted in 90 percent of all public libraries (U.S. Department of Education, National Center for Education Statistics 1995, 16), but most of these are probably story hours for children under the age of five.

In 1987, the Public Library Association published a revision of its planning process. This version defined eight roles that a public library might play in its community and suggested that decision makers select three or four that best fit the community's needs and the library's resources. These primary and secondary roles would then become the focus of the library's service delivery efforts. Only one of these eight roles referred specifically to children; it was labeled Preschoolers' Door to Learning (McClure et al. 1987). The authors of the 1988 planning process argued that all of the other roles could be implemented for all ages, but that service to preschoolers was a unique service for which libraries had no other competitors in local government. As such, it deserved its own role.

The many, many libraries that have declared service to preschoolers to be a formal emphasis implement this function in a number of ways. They have strong parenting and picture book collections. They may provide puppets, educational games, and other realia in addition to books. Library staff may work with nursery schools, Head Start groups, and other early childhood caregivers. And, overwhelmingly, they conduct preschool story hours. The demand in many communities appears to be insatiable, with some libraries reporting attendance of up to 100 children at these programs, which were originally intended to be much more intimate gatherings. A constant thread on the electronic discussion lists for children's librarians is the request for new ideas for preschool story hour programs—finger plays about bats, Hawaiian crafts, flannelboard stories for Halloween—and for new ways to manage the conflict between demand (more programs, bigger audiences) and good practice (more selective programming, smaller audiences).

An emerging trend that I will discuss later is the segmentation of the preschool story hour into special programs for toddlers and infants. Programs that target children younger than the three- and four-year-olds who make up the traditional preschool story hour audience have become very popular with both parents and funding agencies in light of new research findings about emergent literacy and infant brain development.

Looking Ahead

The services discussed in this chapter are provided at most libraries, big and small, regardless of the setting. They have been the basis of children's services for nearly 100 years, and they have worked well. This does not mean, however, that children's librarians can rest on their laurels. The next chapter outlines warning signs that advocates for kids and libraries must heed if they want to be effective for another century.

CHAPTER 3

Warning Signs

WHILE CHILDREN'S LIBRARIANS and the public library directors who support their efforts may feel justly proud of their accomplishments, there are some warning signs that they should heed. We've talked about the good news. Here is the bad news.

Budgetary Shortfalls

Public libraries in the United States are generally funded by local government—cities, counties, townships, and special districts. Hawaii is an exception, with the state funding its local public libraries. Ohio public libraries also receive two-thirds of their funding from the state (Public Library Data Service 1998). As tax-supported institutions, public libraries are subject to changes in the economy that affect tax revenues and to shifts in political ideology that tend to move back and forth across a basically moderate democratic philosophy. When times are good, there is money for libraries. When times are bad, library budgets suffer. Libraries also tend to benefit when political fortune favors spending on education and social welfare programs and to suffer when the politicians are feeling frugal or ideologically less committed to government interventions.

Libraries are sometimes lumped together with other government programs and services in the public mind. When citizens feel cranky about their tax burden and the level of government service they receive, they are likely to vote against library bonds and referenda, as they would against any increase in government spending. In a survey of library referenda for capital construction projects in 1998, Richard B. Hall noted a growing resistance by voters to these measures. He writes, "It would seem that voters are just distrustful of referenda, equating them with the electoral process in general and therefore assuming acceptance puts money into the hands of politicians. Or we may just be experiencing another backlash from citizens tired of shelling out money, even if it is for a cherished institution like their library" (p. 48).

The government trend that most affects public libraries today, says city manager Roger L. Kemp, is the pressure to hold down expenditures. He points out that even though some decision makers firmly believe that public libraries are important to the development of a literate population, an educated citizenry, and a free society, libraries have been underfunded for years. In other words, a belief in the importance of public libraries has not necessarily been translated into budgetary support. He writes, "Because of limited funding and a lower priority when compared to other municipal services, library directors have had to seek community support, private cosponsorship of their programs, and outside funding sources for many services" (1999, 116). Although libraries have been good at finding alternative funding sources for special programs, Kemp says there is still a shortfall in funds for basic services.

It has been encouraging to see the many foundations willing to invest in public library services for children. The DeWitt Wallace-Reader's Digest Fund has underwritten innovative programs in both school and public library programs for young people. Ameritech has sponsored materials and programs in public libraries to acquaint parents with Internet resources for their children. The Carnegie Foundation continues to support public library services for children and young adults. Unfortunately, foundation support does not provide ongoing funding for library programs. Foundations typically provide seed money for demonstration projects or one-time grants to help libraries redress past inequities or to ramp up new programs.

Kemp praises libraries for their use of computers and innovative technology to improve, monitor, and streamline their operations. Other observers, however, have been concerned about the tremendous new costs that information technology has imposed on libraries. Crawford and Gorman, for example, criticize library decision makers who have jumped on one technological bandwagon after another, victims of technolust who assume that the new is always better than the old. They worry about libraries that have become "museums of failed technology," housing successive obsolete technological innovations (1995, 46).

There are signs of health and vitality in the public libraries around the United States. Many big cities—Cleveland, Denver, Los Angeles, San Antonio, and San Francisco, for example—have seen a boom in beautifully designed, lavish central libraries. A nationwide increase in book budgets typically results in the expected increase in book circulation. In general, however, the needs far outstrip the available resources. At a time when children, particularly poor children, have a growing need for the kinds of services libraries can provide, it is terrible to think that a lack of resources might result in a failure to meet those needs.

Shortage of Children's Librarians

Even if budgets for children's library services get a major boost, we might still have trouble finding librarians to provide those services. There is a significant and growing shortage of children's librarians.

The library profession is graying. For many complex reasons—library school closures, cyclical budget crises resulting in hiring freezes, competition from other career choices—we are not replacing ourselves. Concerns about the shortage of professional librarians were at the forefront at a Congress on Professional Education called by the American Library Association in April 1999. One of the delegates to the congress, Marilyn Mason, outgoing director of the Cleveland Public Library, noted with alarm that 75 percent of the professional staff at that library would retire over the next fifteen years (Olson 1999).

There are plenty of jobs for children's librarians. Libraries in Brooklyn, New York, and elsewhere have reinstated the children's specialty position after experimenting for many years with a generalist approach. Others, such as the Sno-Isle System in the state of Washington and the San Francisco Public Library, recently added children's librarians positions. In 1998, Mary Somerville conducted an informal survey of her colleagues in public libraries around the country and found a nationwide shortage of children's librarians. Her respondents indicated many reasons for the shortages: low salaries and amenities, lack of a nearby library school, and the perceived undesirability of a particular library's location, to name a few. The fact is that public libraries seeking children's librarians are competing with many other libraries. It is a seller's market. At the 1999 ALA Annual Conference in New Orleans, the placement center posted 120 job openings in youth services. There were only twenty-eight applicants for those positions (1999Annual Conference placement center stats).

In 1997, only 375, or 23 percent, of the 1,454 new library school graduates reporting job placements went to work for public libraries; this was down from 28 percent the previous year (Gregory and de la Peña McCook 1999). Only ninety-four (7.6 percent) of those 375 new public library job holders indicated a position in youth services. Their salaries ranged from a low of $15,000 to a high of $47,000, with $27,896 being the average and $27,780 the mean salaries. While the high of $47,000 is respectable, the average beginning salary of $27,896 for a youth services librarian compares poorly with the overall average of $30,270. If one compares these starting salaries with those of newly minted MBAs or attorneys, the picture is even more dismal.

Professional Role Strain and Ambiguity

In the spring of 1999, an eleven-year-old boy made national news when he asked the children's librarian at his branch of the San Francisco Public Library if he could volunteer to read to younger children in the library. He planned to wear a wizard suit and motivate the little kids to want to read on their own. He was turned down because it was library policy that only professional children's librarians could read to children. The policy was overturned in this case when Mayor Willie Brown ordered the library to allow the boy his story hour. "Our libraries are supposed to turn kids on, not turn them off," the Mayor told the *San Francisco Chronicle*. "We should be rewarding young people with creative ideas, not discouraging them" (Let boy read 1999, 41).

Much of the expressed public opinion, whipped up by the media, appeared hostile to the library's initial decision not to allow the boy to read aloud to younger children. The retired children's services coordinator, Effie Lee Morris, speaking to a public audience at a library lecture during the controversy, bemoaned the fact that people apparently did not understand the high professional standards that were upheld by children's librarians in the city or the training and skill involved in preparing and conducting a story hour. "They still think that just anybody can read effectively to their children," she said.

Elsewhere, children's librarians have trained volunteers to do some of the tasks that have traditionally been done by professionals. A case in point is the Grandparents and Books (GAB) program that began at Los Angeles Public Library in 1988 with funding from the Library Services and Technology Act (Dowd 1991). Older adults were recruited and trained in the techniques of simple flannelboard storytelling and reading aloud to children. Then the volunteers were deployed to the children's areas during the busy after-school hours. They read to children one on one, freeing the librarians to handle the reference and readers' advisory questions of other children. The program was so successful that the California State Library gave start-up funding to libraries throughout the state to establish their own GAB programs. Today, it's offered in libraries around the country and abroad.

The success of the GAB project seems to rest in the good training it gives to its volunteers and in the mutual satisfaction it brings to both the older adult volunteers and the children. I mention it here to illustrate what may be a new trend—delegating functions once considered the sacred prerogative of the children's librarian to volunteers or paraprofessionals while assigning managerial and supervisory responsibilities to the professional children's librarian. More and more children's librarians, not just those in supervisory or management positions, are training other people to do things they once did themselves.

The result can be role strain. Children's librarians sometimes feel they are giving away the parts of their job that provide the greatest satisfaction even though they recognize that on their own they could never do all the things that should be done to serve the children in their care. They also feel frustrated that their organizations and society at large do not recognize the professional dimension of their work or its intrinsic value. What is the value of a librarian's storytelling skill if an eleven-year-old boy or an elderly volunteer can do it too?

The expanding role of digital information technology as an integral element of public library service to children also presents some librarians with a dilemma. Remember that most librarians see the child as a reader first and the providing of books as their first responsibility. It is often difficult to reconcile this closely held value with the popularity of the public access computers in the children's room. I spent several hours during the summer of 1999 observing the children who use the Children's Center at the new main library in San Francisco. It is an appealing space, occupying its own mezzanine off the atrium in this dramatic building. The information desk is the first thing you see when you walk in the room. It is low, with librarians seated behind it, ready to make eye contact with children as they enter the space. When I was there, however, the great majority of children did not approach the information desk or go to the children's reading room, which is stocked with many good books. Instead, they rushed directly to the Electronic Discovery Center, where twelve computers offer networked CD-ROMs and unfiltered Internet access. A volunteer signed kids up and kept order there. Every computer was in use by at least one child at all times, and the volunteer was kept very busy.

The two librarians at the information desk had much less to do, and they were a little wistful when I asked them about the Electronic Discovery Center. "Yes, it's always busy," they said, "and this is actually a slow day." I asked if the children who use the computers also use the books. "Sometimes," they answered. "More during the school year, when they have homework assignments." How do librarians reconcile their belief in their role as champions for children and books with an everyday reality that privileges children and computers?

Lack of Tangible Outcomes

The ideology on which U.S. public libraries were founded is called the "library faith." This notion that good books will create good citizens who will then create a good society is indeed a matter of faith; there is no proof that this is a valid causal chain. Like motherhood and apple pie, public libraries have been accepted without question as one of the low-priced "goods" in our society. But today, all government services are being asked to demonstrate their accountability. Public officials, elected on platforms of responsible government spending, now routinely ask public institutions to show what kind of bang they produce for their tax-funded bucks. As library operations become more expensive to fund, their perceived worth is more problematic.

I have talked about the effort to document and quantify the products of public library operations through output measures. Public librarians have become expert at counting circulation, reference questions, attendance at programs, and numbers of walk-in patrons. They have even calculated such esoteric measures as "patron fill rates." These output measures have been informative, particularly when used to monitor progress toward goals or to compare performance with earlier benchmark statistics.

Carole Fiore (1998) offers inspiring stories of children's librarians who used statistics successfully to increase their budgets for staff, books, and programs. She also suggests sources of local demographics that are important for librarians to use in planning: the number of babies born in a community, the number of children in day care, elementary school enrollment, the number of homeschooled children, and population forecasts.

Unfortunately, even when librarians carefully quantify their work, they are still unable to document its consequences. They may be able to say with authority that one-third of all preschoolers in their community attended story hours or that, on average, every school-age child checked out fifteen books during the year. They may even be able to demonstrate that this is a 10 percent increase over the year before. What they cannot yet assert with any authority is what difference this made in the lives of those children. This kind of inquiry requires more in-depth data collection, usually longitudinal in nature, and more sophisticated analysis than libraries are capable of carrying out.

Some grant-funded programs have tried to collect data about the outcomes of their work. An example is the Tall Tree Initiative, funded by the DeWitt Wallace-Reader's Digest Foundation, in which third-grade children in one school that participated in the program scored significantly higher on the state reading tests than they had in previous years. The principal attributed at least some of the increase to the influence of the Tall Tree program (Kassin 1999). More rigorous research would help to isolate other contributing variables, but this is still a good preliminary attempt to link tangible outcomes to a library program.

Another interesting effort to quantify the intrinsic benefits of public library service has been centered at the St. Louis Public Library. The library worked with economists for three years to conduct a cost-benefit analysis of the library's return on investment to its public. After analyzing results from several data sources, the researchers determined that every $1 invested in the library produces direct benefits of more than $4. The study team is encouraged by these results and has received funding from the Institute of Museum and Library Services to replicate the study in four other library systems. They hope to validate the results from St. Louis and determine if the methodology can be used elsewhere (Holt and Elliott 1998; Holt, Elliott, and Moore 1999).

Of particular use to children's librarians is the analysis that was done on children's services in St. Louis. The study revealed that while the general return on investment, as noted above, is four to one, users of children's services receive $7 in benefits for every $1 spent by the library. It also determined that people who are most interested in youth services—parents, teachers, and caregivers—place a high dollar value on them. After looking at the data, the library board doubled the size of the children's services training budget and made a commitment to find another $1 million a year in outside funding for youth services (Holt and Holt 1999).

As long as public libraries continue to be subject to market-driven forces, the documentation of quantitative results and outcomes will be important. Good intentions and nostalgia are no longer sufficient justifications for any publicly funded service. It is important to remember, however, that public funding is as much the result of politics as economics. Cost-benefit analyses and monitoring of quantitative results are rational approaches that show a library's ability to use the tools of the market, but children's librarians should not be naïve enough to think that if they can prove their worth with solid statistics, their programs will automatically receive the monetary rewards they have earned. They need to continue to play politics as well as the market.

Public Attacks on Libraries' Technology Policies

Earlier in this book, I noted the high public approval rating that public library service for children has gained. Unfortunately, that motherhood and apple pie shine has begun to tarnish a little with recent highly publicized attacks on libraries' policies of free Internet access. In some people's mind, librarians are purveyors of pornography to children, defending intellectual freedom at the cost of children's innocence.

The challenges began one library at a time, as libraries made the Internet available to the public. Individual protests were followed by legal challenges. The portions of the Communications Decency Act that would have required libraries to use filtering software in order to receive federal funding were struck down as unconstitutional, but legislative efforts to limit the access of minors to the Internet continue. Arizona and South Dakota have passed laws requiring libraries to filter computers that are available to children; similar legislation is pending in Arkansas, California, Florida, Indiana, Minnesota, Oklahoma, Pennsylvania, Virginia, and Wisconsin (Censorship watch 1999, 31).

One of the most frustrating challenges has come from Laura Schlessinger, the Dr. Laura of talk radio fame. She has focused her attack on the American Library Association for linking from its Teen Hoopla Web page to the Go Ask Alice health and sex education site for young people maintained by Columbia University. Schlessinger questions the content of that site, which answers questions raised by young people on such topics as how to prevent gagging during oral sex and how to clean bodily fluids from a cat-o'-nine-tails. She has also criticized Teen Hoopla's link to Peacefire, a youth alliance against Internet censorship. At least one corporate sponsor, Toys "R" Us, withdrew its offer to ALA to fund children's reading rooms in public libraries because of the negative publicity generated by the Schlessinger radio campaign (Dr. Laura crusades 1999, 9-10).

Schlessinger's attacks are not limited to the American Library Association. She has urged listeners to investigate the policies of their local libraries and to hold library budgets hostage until management agrees to protect children from pornography. She has encouraged her listeners to boycott and picket libraries that provide unfiltered Internet access to children.

If these were isolated cases, there would be little cause for alarm, but the challenges to public library policies toward youth appear to be well coordinated. They have been widely publicized and appear to have had some effect on policy makers as well as individual citizens. It is difficult to know how many adults, if any, have decided that the public library is no longer a safe place for children as a result of the current attacks, but efforts by lawmakers to mandate filtering software on public access computers used by children have been increasing.

Perhaps more seriously, parents seem confused by the public libraries' positions on Internet access. "Why don't the libraries want to protect our children?" they ask. The *Orange County Register* recently reported on the range of policies governing public access to the Internet by children and adults at various libraries in southern California. These policies range from filtering all computers at the Yorba Linda Library to the compromise position of requiring parental permission for unrestricted access for minors in the Orange County library system to completely open access at the Newport Beach Public Library.

Two parents with differing perspectives were interviewed. One father insisted that monitoring his son's computer use was his responsibility, not the library's. He had taught his son rules for safety on-line and wasn't worried that the ten-year-old boy might stumble onto something unsavory. "These things may happen," the father said. "It just means he has to be given some additional training." On the other hand, a mother was shocked by a librarian's apparent lack of concern when a patron reported that a boy was peeking at a cybersex Web site. This mother wanted the library to be a safe haven where her daughters could do homework without being exposed to graphic sexual images. She noted that even the local video store kept its X-rated materials off-limits to kids. "What we're asking is for libraries to have the same type of concern for our children—respect for their innocence—that every other establishment seems to have," she said (Chmielewski 1999, 9).

Many lay people are confused or unconvinced by the intellectual freedom argument made by professional librarians. I spent a long time recently talking to a man, a grandfather, who was looking for someone to speak to his service club about public libraries and Internet access. In many ways, he represents the point of view of average concerned citizens. He is a rational man who has made a considerable effort to inform himself about the complex issues involved. While he agrees that parents should ultimately be responsible for this and all other matters relating to their kids, he told me, "I still think you librarians are wrong about this. It's like guns. Kids shouldn't have the right to bear arms, and they shouldn't have the right to find smut on the Internet. We adults need to protect them from themselves." He believes that the library's status as a public tax-funded agency makes it even more important that the institution put protection of children ahead of the more abstract concept of intellectual freedom.

A few librarians also oppose the application of strict First Amendment principles to the Internet. David Burt, a public librarian from Oregon, is an outspoken proponent of Internet software filters. Through Filtering Facts, a nonprofit organization that promotes the use of filtering software to shield children from pornography, he has waged a dogged campaign against ALA's opposing position on filtering and against specific public libraries that have resisted his efforts to impose software filters. In October 1999, he named the "ten most unsafe public libraries for children," all large library systems that have avoided the use of filtering software (Filtering Facts Friday Letter).

Changing Lives of Children

Perhaps the warning sign that librarians should pay most attention to is the change that is occurring in the ways children experience their lives today. Childhood is itself a social construct that changes over time as societies and cultures change (Aries 1962; Demos 1986; Sommerville 1982). In the next chapter I will explore some of the significant changes that are affecting the lives of the children who use our libraries and those we would like to serve. Social and technological changes are having profound impacts on how children live their lives and how society perceives them. If libraries are going to be a part of the social and cultural fabric of children's lives in the twenty-first century, they must respond to these changes in positive ways.

The Changing Lives of Children

RAPID CHANGE HAS BECOME a defining characteristic of American life in the twenty-first century. It affects how we do our jobs, spend our time, and raise our families. The lives of children have also changed in many ways over the last quarter of a century. In this chapter I will discuss how changes in the structure and fabric of society affect the children we want to serve in our libraries.

Thinking about Change

Why do we focus so intensely on change as we move into the new millennium? Wasn't change a hallmark of the twentieth century? Shouldn't we be used to it by now?

The technology and media observer Douglas Rushkoff points out that the change we are experiencing now is different in several important ways from the normal evolutionary change in human society. Certainly the rate of change, facilitated by rapid advancements in technology, is faster than it has ever been. Rushkoff writes, "Today's 'screenager'—the child born into a culture mediated by television and computers—is interacting with his world in at least as dramatically altered a fashion from his grandfather as the first sighted creature did from his blind ancestors, or a winged one from his earthbound forebears" (1996, 3). Rushkoff points out that the technology-driven change we are experiencing also tends to be nonlinear and nonprogressive, hence unpredictable and often threatening to those of us who like to feel in control. He is optimistic about our future, however, and suggests that we follow the lead of the children who are immigrating successfully into the future. The children, he claims, are the advance scouts for an unknown future. They are developing the adaptive skills for a life of constantly changing cultural, social, and technological environments. They are already, he says, "the thing that we must become" (p. 13).

Historian Gary Cross offers another perspective on the discontinuity that comes with the turbulent change of our time. In his fascinating social history of American toys, *Kids' Stuff* (1997), he argues that toys have traditionally reflected parents' hopes for their children. At the beginning of the twentieth century, these were usually very gender-specific hopes. Boys were given erector sets and other sophisticated construction toys that would introduce them to the world of technology, while girls were given dolls to mother. Both boys and girls were given blocks to develop their fine motor skills. Toy manufacturers and retailers still tend to market their products along gender lines, as anyone who has walked the aisles of Toys "R" Us or purchased a Happy Meal at McDonald's is aware.

In the 1930s, toy manufacturers began to appeal directly to kids with toys based on childhood fantasies and mass media heroes such as Shirley Temple and Buck Rogers. Television advertising ratcheted up the campaign for the kids' market dramatically. Now, Cross claims, after their children's preschool years most parents no longer think about the educational value of a toy or how a toy might prepare their child for the future. They are more concerned with gratifying a child's craving for the latest craze than with the quality of the child's interaction with the toy.

Toys no longer mark the child's passage from one age to another or even the observance of special holidays such as Christmas, although that is still a blockbuster time for toy companies. The popular toys of childhood are now the toys of popular child culture, cleverly conceived and marketed by adults, of course. Cross speculates that in this time of rapid change, parents no longer know what kind of future to prepare their children for, and this has changed the meaning of childhood in some important ways. He explains, "When toys lost their connection to the experience and expectations of parents, they entered a realm of ever-changing fantasy. Indeed, the parent's gift to the child increasingly became not the learning of the future or reason or even the sharing of a joy of childhood. Parents instead granted children the right to participate in a play world of constant change without much guidance or input from adults" (p. 227). If Cross is right, it is a telling commentary when parents are so accustomed to change that they dare not make assumptions about their children's future.

In order to keep up with the rapid pace of life itself, Americans find themselves getting busier and busier. In a world where "multitasking" is considered a survival skill, even children's lives are becoming more organized, with less leisure time for the idle play that was once considered their birthright. A study conducted at the University of Michigan tracked children for thirty years. Using 1981 as a benchmark for comparison with 1997, the researchers found that children today spend eight more hours a week in school (because of increasing participation in preschool, not the lengthening of the elementary school day), two hours more in organized sports, forty-five minutes more studying, and three more hours on household work than they did sixteen years ago. They watch less TV than they used to and spend more than two hours less playing during a typical week. Free time represented 40 percent of a child's weekday hours in 1981; it had shrunk to 25 percent by 1997, and kids had to fit studying and housework into that limited time. On average, children in 1997 were reading for pleasure only seventy-seven minutes a week (Healy, M. 1998).

Inevitably, adults worry that children today are growing up too fast, being pushed into the stressful pace of adult life much too early. A recent *Newsweek* article about the lives of children between the ages of eight and fourteen described them as a "generation stuck on fast forward" (Kantrowitz and Wingert 1999, 64.) One ten-year-old girl who is profiled in the article worries about the three hours of homework she has to do each night, about homelessness, and about classmates who are already starting to date. "My life is really hectic right now," she says. "I'm already doing what some people in the 1800s weren't doing until they were full-grown adults. I get up at 6:30 every morning, go to school and have to rush through all my classes, come home and work on my homework, go to ice-skating lessons, watch a little TV, talk on the phone, do more homework and practice my violin. If I'm lucky, I get to sleep by eleven. And then the entire ordeal starts again" (p. 65). Her mother says this is what it's like to be a child of the nineties. Librarians might wonder when or why this child would ever find time to visit the local library or read a book for pleasure.

The Impact of Digital Technology

Don Tapscott (1998) calls them the Net Generation. They are the offspring of the baby boomers, the children who are growing up with the Internet. Tapscott is convinced that these young people are being formed by their involvement with digital media and are in turn influencing many aspects of our society—entertainment, schooling, commerce, perhaps even government.

According to Nicholas Negroponte (1995), the founding director of the media lab at the Massachusetts Institute of Technology, the emerging digital world is both irrevocable and unstoppable, and the rate of change is unprecedented. Certainly the rate of adoption of digital technology in homes, schools, and libraries has been more rapid than anyone could have predicted. A report compiled by the Children's Partnership (1999) found that 25 percent of all U.S. households now have Internet access and that households with children are more likely to be connected than those with adults only. Sixty percent of all U.S. homes with children between the ages of eight and seventeen have computers, and 61 percent of those homes have Internet access. As of July 1998, 16 million American kids, about one in four, were on-line. About half (55 percent) of the children ages eleven and older used the Internet for their schoolwork. The young people Tapscott studied, teenagers between thirteen and nineteen, were the most avid of all Internet users, regardless of age.

Unfortunately, the rapid penetration of computers into American households has raised issues of equity. The same Children's Partnership report notes that only 2 percent of children in low-income rural households have Internet access, compared with 50 percent of the young people in urban households with incomes over $75,000. Income is probably a factor in the disparity between computers in households headed by female, single parents (25 percent) and in two-parent households (57 percent). There is also a racial divide in computer and Internet availability: 40.8 percent of all white households have computers, and 21.2 percent are connected to the Internet, but only 19.3 percent of African American households and 19.4 percent of Hispanic households have computers. Fewer than 10 percent of those households have Internet access. Poverty is a major deciding factor, of course. Only 8 percent of low-income families have Internet access at home (Bennetts 1999, 92).

Schools compensate for some of the inequities in access to digital technology. By the fall of 1998, 89 percent of all public schools were connected to the Internet; and 51 percent of all instructional rooms (classrooms, libraries, and computer labs) were wired. David Tyack and Larry Cuban, scholars of educational reform, note that computers have spread far more rapidly in schools than any previous form of educational technology. Huge amounts of money have been invested to accomplish this—more than a billion dollars between 1984 and 1992. Nonetheless, they observe, these computers are rarely integrated into classroom practices or the overall curriculum. Most students who use computers at school use them only an hour a week (1995, 125). Unfortunately, Internet access in schools also correlates strongly with income and education levels in the communities they serve (Coley, Cradler, and Engel 1997). The very children who are unlikely to have computers at home are also unlikely to have them at school.

Public libraries also make computers and the Internet available to children as well as adults. The 1998 survey of U.S. public library Internet connectivity conducted by the American Library Association's Office for Information Technology Policy concluded that 73.3 percent of all public libraries offer public access to the Internet. Presumably this access is not limited to adults. The authors of the study note that nearly every public library has or is developing an acceptable use policy governing their patron access to the Internet, and about one in seven libraries use filters on some or all of their computer workstations (Bertot and McClure 1998).

Public library access is particularly important as a means of addressing the digital divide between information haves and have-nots. An update on Internet equity issues from the Benton Foundation (Becht, Taglang, and Wilhelm 1999) cites several recent studies showing that African Americans and Hispanics are more likely to use computers and the Internet in locations other than homes, including public libraries. This suggests that public libraries have a significant mission in addressing issues of equity of access to information technology. I recently observed children using the Electronic Discovery Center at the San Francisco Public Library and found that the city's poorest and most diverse children were indeed using the computers there in large numbers. While unaccompanied children accounted for most of the after-school and summertime users, there were also many adults who watched with pride as their children or grandchildren entered the Information Age.

In spite of the prevailing hype about kids and computers, adults have mixed opinions about the benefit of the Internet, with its untrammeled access to a chaotic wealth of information, for children. Advocates like Dan Tapscott, mentioned above, see the Internet as a liberating and empowering vehicle for children to build community, learn at their own pace and in accordance with their own learning styles, and generate as well as receive information on any conceivable subject, which, of course, is precisely what some adults worry about. Gary Marchionini and Herman Maurer (1995) point enthusiastically to a digital world in which teachers and students have access to information resources that had been physically and conceptually inaccessible to them in the past. They describe the benefits of virtual field trips and virtual guest speakers, available to all children in all classrooms everywhere. In fact, the rapid digitization of many primary source materials is making archival information that was previously inaccessible available to Internet users of all ages (Thomas 1998).

One of the early gurus of computing for children, Seymour Papert (1993), was convinced that computers, used properly, could engage children in constructivist activities in which they could learn through creative problem-solving tasks. He was also optimistic about the computer's potential for enabling teachers to work more effectively with children's different learning styles. A good example of this is the eighth-grade classroom in Long Beach where low-income, first-generation immigrant children are creating Web pages for local businesses and other schools in the district (Shuit 1998). Papert has been concerned, however, about the tendency for many untrained teachers to settle for "drill-and-kill" computer applications that dampen students' natural enthusiasm for what he calls "the children's machine."

Detractors also worry about children's privacy, sexual predators, access to inappropriate materials, and possible negative effects on children's social and intellectual development. In a study conducted by the Annenberg Public Policy Center at the University of Pennsylvania (1999), 75 percent of the parents surveyed said they think the Internet is a good place for children to explore and discover fascinating things and 72 percent believe it helps children with their schoolwork, but 78 percent also worry that their children might give away personal information or view sexually explicit material. It is this mixed potential of the Internet that makes it such an explosive policy issue.

One of the more devastating critiques of the educational and developmental value of computer use by children was issued recently by Jane Healy (1998), an educational psychologist. Citing a number of studies and her own observations, she argues that schools are subjecting children to an optimistic experiment when they hook kids up to computers. She points out that there is no proof, or even convincing evidence, that it will work. She worries that the edutainment products being promoted for home and classroom use do not encourage true learning. This true learning requires students to make connections between facts and ideas, and it is often hard work. Most of the educational CD-ROMs in use just require children to access isolated information or to exercise routine skills. At worst, they may even foster dangerous habits of mind—impulsivity, trial-and-error guessing over thoughtful problem solving, a disregard for consequences, and the expectation of easy pleasure (pp. 53-54). Yasmin Kafai (1993) echoes this concern, pointing out that much of the software currently available for children is boring or pointless. Many poorly designed edutainment products promote mindless point-and-click activities or simply retrieve isolated, decontextualized bits of information. Like Papert, Kafai would rather see children using computers as tools, developing their own computer games or producing their own digital portfolios for classroom use.

Another dimension to children's use of digital technology is the effect of gender. It seems clear that at this time in the development of the technology, boys and girls use computers differently. Teachers, librarians, and parents everywhere notice the same phenomenon: Boys clamor to get to the computers; girls need to be enticed. Girls typically start school with less technological experience than boys and demonstrate less confidence in their ability to use computers than boys do (Vail 1997). Research shows that even in kindergarten, both boys and girls agree that boys like playing with computers more than girls do. Boys' fascination with the computer continues into adulthood, where men dominate the high-tech industries (Cassell and Jenkins 1998). When older girls take computer classes, they are more likely to gravitate to courses in data entry and word processing than the higher-end courses in programming (AAUW 1998).

Boys are particularly enthusiastic about cyberspace games, from the relatively benign to the more violent products such as Doom and Quake, which achieved notoriety as the computer games of choice for the young killers in Littleton, Colorado (Braun 1999). The developers of software and computer games for the home market have aimed their products primarily at boys, who already have demonstrated their passion for the fast response and manic action of video games.

Recently, however, some software developers began to specialize in products for girls. Barbie Fashion Designer, which reportedly sold half a million units in its first two months, may have piqued their interest (Subrahmanyam and Greenfield 1998). The founders of Purple Moon conducted their own research before launching their first two CD-ROMs for girls in 1997. They found that girls are "horizontal competitors," more interested in figuring out their opponents than in outwitting them or establishing power over them. Because girls are interested in social relationships, Purple Moon has conceived its CD-ROMs as "friendship adventures." Rockett's New School focuses on social situations, while Secret Paths in the Forest generates more private, imaginative play. Both of these products are richly textured multimedia environments with enhanced audio effects and imaginative graphics, features that girls find appealing (Purple Moon 1997). There is no evidence, however, that Purple Moon's gentle CD-ROMs are even close to outselling the violent and popular boys' games, in spite of a marketing campaign designed especially to attract girls and their mothers (Interview with Brenda Laurel 1998).

Girls, with their higher verbal abilities and passion for social connections, also respond eagerly to e-mail and chat functions. Boys prefer the role-playing MUD and MOO sites and action games. In one high school, the librarian and the technology coordinator found that the best way to encourage gender equity in the computer labs was to prohibit games and encourage e-mail accounts (Jacobson 1998).

The Future of Books in a Digital Age

Will kids still read books at the end of the twenty-first century? Lacking a crystal ball, I am unwilling to predict. However, children are likely to encounter what Eliza Dresang (1997; 1999) calls the "handheld book" for many years to come. Douglas Rushkoff thinks that the experience of reading and using digital data is making computer users value the printed medium even more highly because of its unique properties. He explains, "More than mere holders of data, printed media are tangible objects with texture and weight, providing a sense of a physical connection to the writer and subject" (1996, 111). He does note, however, that the stories that most appeal to young people are increasingly nonlinear, like the digital media themselves (p. 66).

Books themselves may be changing to reflect the new media of the digital age. Dresang (1999) writes convincingly about the evidence for such "radical change" in literature for young people today. She finds three dimensions of change in contemporary children's literature:

> changing forms and formats that reflect the nonlinear aspects of hypertext-based media, changing perspectives that reflect the multiple voices available to children through television and the World Wide Web

> changing boundaries that reflect new subjects, new settings, new ways
> to present character, and a new tolerance for ambiguity.

It is impossible to tell whether these changes are the result of influences on writers and illustrators of children's books or if they reflect an awareness that children's interests, tastes, and ways of processing information have changed. In either case, the resulting literary output is extraordinary and may herald a new golden age in literature for children and young adults.

Whether children will have the skills to read the creative content of the handheld book is another question. Overall, reading scores are holding their own and even improving slightly. However, the percentage of fourth-grade students across the country who scored below the basic reading level in 1998 is a frightening 39 percent (Annie E. Casey Foundation 1999). When the scores are broken down by race, they are even more disturbing. At all three grades tested by the National Assessment of Educational Progress in 1998— fourth, eighth, and twelfth—white students tested higher than children of color. Low-income children who were eligible for the federally funded free lunch programs performed at lower levels than those who were not eligible (Donahue et al. 1999). The same children cited in studies as having limited access to digital information technology appear also to have less access to print. Poverty is a telling factor in putting kids at risk for educational failure.

Disparities in test scores and uneasiness about the effectiveness of public education in general have led to a sometimes-virulent battle over schooling.

The Battle over Schooling

The cover of the *New York Times Magazine* on June 14, 1998, featured a school desk chair and a multiple-choice question that asked what it represented. The possible responses were (a) a charter school desk, (b) the latest capitalist tool, (c) a way to empower poor parents, (d) the next great battleground, (e) all of the above. The answer, of course, was (e) all of the above. The accompanying article on school choice (Winerip) laid out the complex issues surrounding this particular approach to school reform, all of which are implied by the multiple-choice answers indicated above.

Like public libraries, public schools have really not changed that much since the turn of the century in their basic organization and mission, particularly in large urban settings. Diane Ravitch and Joseph P. Vitteriti (1997), both critics of public education, describe the traditional urban public school as a "factory model," designed on scientific management principles for maximum efficiency. They acknowledge its early success in educating large numbers of immigrants who became literate and productive members of American society. In the industrial economy of the early twentieth century, children who never enrolled in school or who left without graduating were usually able to find a job that did not require a high school education, sometimes at good wages. Unfortunately, the factory model, designed to process large numbers of students, no longer works so well.

The educational requirements of the contemporary labor market are much more rigorous than they were before World War II. The low-skill, high-wage jobs of the traditional industrial economy no longer exist. When educational economists Richard Murnane and Frank Levy (1996) compared the labor needs of the current economy with the educational achievement of seventeen-year-old Americans, they concluded that schools are no longer teaching the skills that are needed in the workforce. They prescribed curricular reform that would emphasize the "hard" skills, which are basic math, problem solving, and high-level reading skills; the "soft" skills of working in groups and oral and written communications; and the ability to use a personal computer for simple tasks such as word processing.

The bureaucracies that were developed to manage large urban school districts have in many instances become rigid and unresponsive to students, parents, and teachers as well as to the needs of the workplace. Like the early twentieth-century immigrants who flocked to big city schools, the child immigrants of today are often poor and limited in their ability to speak English. They are also more at risk than those earlier immigrants because of social dislocation, community disorder or violence, and health problems. It is a sad irony that many families fled wars in their homelands only to find that their new American communities are not the safe havens they were expecting.

Two researchers who studied the situation also remind us that unlike the earlier wave of immigrants, today's immigrant children are overwhelmingly non-European. They are much less homogeneous than the immigrant populations who came to this country a hundred years ago; their national origins, culture, socioeconomic backgrounds, and legal status are astonishingly diverse (Rong and Preissle 1998). These new immigrants do not respond as readily to old patterns of assimilation and conventional English language education.

In Minneapolis, for example, at least 8,400 of the district's 50,000 students didn't speak English as their first language during the 1998-1999 school year. Hundreds of Somali families recently resettled there to escape the civil war in their country, and teachers are struggling with cultural differences and language difficulties in communicating with children who have spent the last year in Kenyan refugee camps. One first-grade teacher who admits to never having seen an African American person himself until he was in the eighth grade talked about his struggles to learn how to teach children raised by strict Muslim families in a war-torn land. "How am I going to communicate with these children? Am I going to offend them?" he muses (Taylor 1999, A8). At least this teacher is aware of the implications of cultural differences for his students' educational achievement; not all educators are that sensitive.

School Reform

The movement for school reform is thus a response to some very real problems, particularly in our urban schools. Specific reforms such as charter schools, site-based management, and school choice have been advocated and implemented to some degree.

Charter schools are public schools operated under a charter, or contract, between the group or individuals operating the school and a sponsor such as a state or local school board. Louann Bierlein (1997) has observed that, in principle, charter schools focus on results rather than inputs because their charters ordinarily require that they meet a certain level of student achievement. This mandate for accountability appeals to advocates of a more consumer-driven educational system.

Some critics of charter schools say they are a device for distracting the public from more broad-based and systemic reforms or that they are the first step toward school vouchers. Others are concerned that charter schools will lead to resegregation or to elitist schools that educate a few privileged children at the public's expense. Teachers unions have fought charter schools because their autonomy and their emphasis on results have led some of these schools to hire noncredentialed teachers. Some research indicates that existing charter schools actually serve a higher proportion of African American, Hispanic, and Native American children than do other public schools (Bierlein 1997, 51.) The charter school movement is still too new and too small to yield much dependable data about its potential for large-scale reform, but it has already challenged some long-held assumptions about public schools and has served as laboratories for experimentation in curriculum, teaching methods, and parental involvement.

Site-based management is a reform strategy that aims to break down the centralized authority of bureaucratized school systems and to return decision-making powers to the school site itself. It aims to enhance school performance by giving more control to the local school community—administrators, teachers, parents, and sometimes other community members or stakeholders. The degree of autonomy granted to the local site varies considerably, and the schools are still bound by the collective bargaining contracts and overall curriculum decisions of the parent jurisdiction. However, in some cases, the local school may decide how money is spent—on the school library or an arts program, for example—and most site-based management programs emphasize local decisions about hiring and teaching methods.

One study of school-based management reported that the most successful efforts distributed decision-making powers broadly through a network of teams at the site. These effective schools invested heavily in professional development that gave their participants the skills in teamwork, budgeting, curriculum, and instruction needed to implement the reform, and they developed incentive systems that rewarded individuals for their participation. They collected data about student, staff, and school performance that enabled them to monitor their progress toward educational goals. They shared a vision of educational excellence that guided their work (Wohlstetter et al. 1997). Like other forms of participative management, this strategy is time- and labor-intensive. Some teachers resent the time it takes from classroom teaching and preparation, but others thrive in an environment that values their opinions about curriculum and educational practice. Parent involvement is also required for site-based management. This is usually a benefit for all involved, although some teachers and administrators find parent participants to be uninformed and intrusive.

School choice is probably the most controversial of the school reforms being considered today. It has been linked closely to political agendas on the left and right, and it is the strategy that is most resisted by the education establishment. The classic public school model postulates children attending their neighborhood schools, but that model was upset during the 1960s, when busing was devised as a strategy for integrating urban schools. In cities where housing discrimination and other social forces produced racially segregated neighborhoods, attending a neighborhood school usually meant attending a segregated school. When the courts mandated that schools be integrated, many urban school districts responded by assigning children to schools according to formulas for racial balance, using buses to transport students from their own neighborhoods to the schools.

Obviously, busing was not designed as an exercise in school choice; it was involuntary in most cases. However, some school districts that were faced with court-ordered busing, including the Los Angeles Unified School District, tried to create opportunities for parental choice by designing "magnet" schools with attractive programs that would entice parents to send their children there. Enrollments at the magnet schools were determined by racial quotas. While busing has been abandoned in Los Angeles because of successful legal challenges by angry parents, the magnet schools still exist and offer some limited choice to parents who want to shop for their children's schools.

Open enrollment is a moderate form of school choice. School systems with open enrollment policies allow parents to enroll their children in any school that has open slots, regardless of its location. The hope is that market pressures will force schools to perform at levels that will enable them to compete in the marketplace of parental consumers. Schools showing decreased enrollment will receive less funding, and those with increases in enrollment will do better in the budget game.

In Seattle, Washington, where an open enrollment plan recently replaced 20 years of an integration-driven busing program, schools find themselves actively marketing their programs in order to recruit students who will drive up their numbers and their funding base. The Seattle reform effort combines its open enrollment policies with many elements of site-based management, encouraging each school to make decisions about programs and pedagogy. One school in an upscale neighborhood published a brochure that promoted its low class sizes, $250,000 technology grant, and high fourth-grade test scores. A school with slipping enrollment figures decided to offer two full-day kindergarten classes to attract working parents. A school with a strong performing arts program highlighted its award-winning chorus in a series of public performances (Murphy 1998).

Voucher systems, the most controversial form of school choice, are primarily a hypothetical option because they have been implemented only on a limited scale. In their purest form, they would give the parents of every school-age child a voucher that would enable them to "purchase" a basic level of education at any school they choose—public, private, or parochial. Several areas have implemented limited voucher plans.

In 1990, 1,000 low-income children in Milwaukee, Wisconsin, were given vouchers that allowed their families to choose from among several private secular schools. As might be expected, opponents of voucher plans—the Carnegie Foundation for the Advancement of Teaching and the president of the American Federation of Teachers—found no measurable gains in the learning outcomes for students who participated in the program. On the other hand, writers in more conservative publications such as *Public Interest* and the *Wall Street Journal* found benefits, including cost savings, in the private schools (Peterson and Noyes 1997).

A federal judge halted a more comprehensive voucher program in Ohio just eighteen hours before public schools were due to open in 1999. School choice extended here to parochial schools, and the judge found that the tax-payer-financed scholarships for low-income students violated mandates for separation of church and state (Judge halts vouchers 1999). Wider adoption of voucher programs would require some significant shifts in constitutional interpretations and public attitudes toward public education.

The Controversy over Bilingual Education

Almost 2.5 million school children in the United States have difficulty speaking English, up from 1.3 million in 1979. Overall, the number of limited-English-speaking children is 5 percent of the school-age population. In some regions of the country, however, the percentage is considerably higher (Federal Interagency Forum on Child and Family Statistics 1999, 6). Most of the children in the United States who speak a language other than English at home are Hispanic.

Bilingual education has been one of the school reforms designed to ensure that non-English-speaking children would learn basic skills at the same time that they mastered the English language. A recent report on children's reading issued by the National Research Council found that trying to teach non-English-speaking children to read in English produces poor results because these students are unable to distinguish the sounds of the language that underlie the written structure. They also have difficulty reading for meaning because they don't understand either the language or the references in the texts. The researchers recommended that children who arrive at school without English proficiency be taught how to read in their native language whenever possible (National Research Council 1998, 324-25).

This practice of bilingual instruction has been challenged on both political and educational grounds. Some of the attacks on bilingual education have been linked to anti-immigration sentiments, but even some leaders within the Hispanic community claim that bilingual education has failed to teach children the skills they need to survive and compete in an English-speaking society. Within the educational community, some critics argue that bilingual education has not produced the desired effects and that children are not transitioning to English early enough or mastering the basic skills sufficiently.

The politics surrounding Proposition 227, the anti-bilingual education initiative that passed overwhelmingly in California in 1998, were fascinating. Funded largely by a white millionaire who claimed to be concerned about the educational achievement of children who don't learn English, the initiative was opposed by almost all bilingual teachers and many Latino leaders and advocacy groups. Polls showed, however, that it was supported by 62 percent of registered Latino voters (La Ganga 1998). A similar division within the Hispanic community has been reported in Denver and Albuquerque, where citizens have also launched political attacks on existing bilingual programs (Sahagun 1998).

Most experts agree that being truly bilingual, fluent in two languages, is an asset to any individual. Losing a native language, on the other hand, can be traumatic for a child and disruptive to an immigrant family. In many newcomer families, the child is the first—and sometimes the only—person to become fluent in English. As long as the children can still speak their mother tongue, they are often called upon to translate for their parents and mediate many of the intricacies of life in this English-speaking country. This can create problems of generational role reversal as the parents become dependent on the children and the children take on adult responsibilities much too early. Another set of problems occurs when children lose their native language and can no longer communicate with their monolingual parents (Rong and Preissle 1998).

Perhaps the example of Miami, Florida, is a good one for other urban areas to consider. There the business community, eager to hire skilled workers who are fluent in English as well as Spanish, has fueled an approach that conceptualizes bilingual education as enrichment rather than as a remedial intervention (Anderson 1998).

The Controversy over Curriculum and Teaching Methods

Most of the initiatives and controversies related to school reform and bilingual education have been concentrated in urban areas where the schools are demonstrably less effective in educating diverse students. More homogeneous and well-financed suburban schools have not escaped the education wars, however. Elementary schools throughout the country have had to contend with divisive debate over "best practices" and methods for teaching core subjects as well as the content of the curriculum itself.

Reading instruction has been a particularly thorny subject. To the layperson, it often appears that the education establishment embraces one fad after another, from "look-say" to phonics to whole language and back again. Experts disagree about which fad to embrace, with phonics and whole language approaches apparently on a collision course.

If it is heeded by educational policy makers, a recent report from the National Research Council could resolve the issue as it applies to teaching basic reading skills to young children. After examining copious research studies on language and literacy acquisition, reading achievement, and reading instruction, the expert panel determined that young children must master three basic accomplishments before they arrive at school to begin formal reading instruction.

First, they need oral language skills and phonological awareness. Phonological awareness is not phonics, but rather an ability to think about how words sound, apart from what they mean. Children who have a requisite level of phonological awareness can hear the two syllables in a word like "chicken" and hear the rhymes in "cat" and "hat." Second, children who are ready to learn to read are motivated to learn and already appreciate the forms of literature. They have heard appealing stories read to them, have watched grownups around them read for information and for pleasure, and are eager to read themselves. Finally, they are aware of the conventions of print and can recognize letters. If all children could start first grade with these skills, teachers would be able to concentrate on word recognition and comprehension, the basic elements of reading mastery (National Research Council 1999). In other words, reading instruction that begins in infancy and combines elements of *both* phonics and whole language is the most likely to be effective.

Will this definitive report from a body as prestigious as the National Research Council put this controversy about methods for teaching reading to rest? Probably not. Tyack and Cuban (1995) note that the history of education in the United States has been a history of cycles of proposals to improve schools and thus to improve society. They speculate that these cycles result from deep conflicts of values and interests that are intrinsic to public education. In particular, the history of school reform reflects the tensions between democratic politics, with its values on access and equality, and the pressures of a competitive market economy. They point out that policy elites, as represented by the National Research Council, have always dominated the discourse on school reform, but the public has not always felt easy about the results.

Public libraries have felt pressure for some time from fundamentalist parents who want to see books about creationism on the shelves next to the books about evolution and dinosaurs. Some library patrons would like to see no books about evolution in the collections. Schools also experience the crossfire between the scientific community and the religious right. The Kansas Board of Education recently voted to discourage the teaching of evolution and to eliminate the topic of the Big Bang from the scientific community completely. With this decision they joined the state of Alabama, which, according to an article the *New York Times*, prints a warning in all of its science books stating that: "This textbook discusses evolution, a controversial theory some scientists present as a scientific explanation for the origin of living things, such as plants, animals, and humans. No one was present when life first appeared on Earth. Therefore, any statements about life's origins should be considered as theory, not fact" (Johnson 1999). Librarians have traditionally resisted such labeling practices.

Homeschooling

Some parents have opted out of the institutional school battlefield altogether and are educating their children at home. What started out as a fringe movement among fundamentalist Christian and antiestablishment left-wing parents is now moving into the mainstream. While the actual numbers are elusive, the best estimate is that more than 1.5 million children are now homeschooled in the United States (Kantrowitz and Wingert 1998, 66). The motivations to teach children at home are varied. Some parents get into homeschooling because they are concerned about public school safety; others worry about secular influences on their children. Some have children with learning disabilities or emotional problems; others have children with unusual talents, intelligence, or creative gifts. The Internet has been a rich resource for many homeschooling families looking for curriculum aids or information to support learning needs. The public library has been another resource.

Hopefully, the turmoil over schooling will result in better educational experiences for children. Some of the reform efforts are motivated by a genuine desire to create more effective learning environments, but others are motivated by political agendas of people with little real concern for children.

Change and controversy in schools affect public libraries as well as school libraries. Children's librarians scramble to anticipate and respond to changes in curriculum with appropriate changes in collection emphases. In communities beset by curriculum wars, librarians debate the merits of placing creationist books alongside the books on evolution, and they search for appropriate phonics texts. Where school districts have implemented year-round schools, children's librarians have adapted their traditional summer reading programs to the needs of year-round students. In urban areas where few children attend their neighborhood schools, children's librarians visit classrooms to promote library usage in general rather than usage of the school's local library.

Living in a Multicultural, Multiracial Society

In 1950, 87.5 percent of American children were white; 11.6 percent were African American, and .9 percent were other nonwhite. By 1980, the United States had begun to move away from being a predominantly white nation with its strongest roots in European culture to a much more diverse and multicultural society. By 1995, only 68.7 percent of American children were white. African American children were 15.3 percent of the youth population; 11.3 percent were Hispanic children, primarily Mexican American; 3.8 percent were Asian/Pacific Islander; and .9 percent were American Indian, Eskimo, or Aleut. Because of trends in birth rates and immigration patterns, the percentage of children who are Hispanic and Asian/Pacific Islander is expected to continue increasing as the number of white and African American children decreases (Sanders and Mattson 1998, 16). Demographers at the Annie E. Casey Foundation (1999) project an overall 4 percent increase in the number of children in the United States from 1997 to 2005. Their computations lead them to believe that the number of white children will decrease by 3 percent during this period, while the numbers of African American, Hispanic, and Asian/Pacific Islander children will all increase, Hispanics and Asian/Pacific Islanders dramatically.

It is understandable, given these demographic figures, that library users would also be more diverse than they have been in the past. Indeed, more than 40 percent of the public libraries responding to a national survey in

1994 reported that their children and young adult patrons were more diverse than they had been five years previously. In urban metropolitan libraries, the number was even higher, with 57 percent reporting increased diversity in the children using their libraries (U.S. Department of Education, National Center for Education Statistics 1995, 5).

Attitudes about the increasing diversity of our population have shifted since the early part of the century, when the inequality between racial groups was taken for granted and those who could were expected to be assimilated into the American melting pot along with the waves of European immigrants before them. Current public rhetoric and policies reflect a more "politically correct" awareness of the value of ethnic and racial diversity and a greater sensitivity to the damage created by stereotyping. It is instructive that Crayola, the venerable manufacturer of crayons used by generations of school children announced in 1999 that for only the third time in its history it would change the name of a Crayola color—from "Indian red" to "chestnut." The two earlier name changes had been from "Prussian blue" to "midnight blue" in 1958, presumably because children no longer understood the original reference, and from "flesh" to "peach" in 1962, because even the casual observer could tell that human flesh came in more than one tone (Py-Lieberman 1999).

The increasing diversity of the children who are the actual and potential users of public libraries raises a number of issues about the collections we develop and the services we offer. Elsewhere I talk about efforts to make library materials collections more reflective of the diverse communities we serve. There is relatively little research and only minimal anecdotal evidence, however, about strategic initiatives to make library services more responsive to the needs of a multicultural population of children.

Professor Clara Chu (1999), at UCLA's Department of Information Studies, has been conducting research on immigrant children who, because of their relatively more developed English language skills, act as the information seekers in the English-speaking world for their entire families. She finds that these immigrant children mediators, as she calls them, are called on to seek a wide range of information on behalf of their parents. The most widely reported information needs were education, medical services, home repairs, recreation, entertainment, and travel. These young people are also asked to find information for their parents on jobs, immigration, taxes, legal matters, business opportunities, banking, car repairs, transportation, and emergency or safety issues. In doing so, the children are required to interpret or translate for their parents, fill out forms, ask questions, write letters, and obtain specific services. Children as young as five engage in these activities.

Chu found that 96 percent of the seventy-seven immigrant children she studied did not use the library as a source of information. Many thought the library was just for reading, studying, or homework or that the library didn't have the kind of information they would need to help their parents. Their most used information resource, incidentally, was the telephone book.

In a follow-up study, Chu asked thirty-three librarians to consider what libraries might do to help immigrant children handle their information transactions. The librarians suggested a number of services they could provide, including classes to introduce these young people to useful information sources, more proactive acquisition of the kind of practical information the children apparently need, partnerships with other community service organizations who serve the same immigrant families, more targeted marketing of services to immigrant children, more bilingual family programming for immigrant families, and staff development to raise awareness of the needs of this group of potential library users. In most cases, unfortunately, the librarians' responses indicated desirable services rather than services that were already in place.

Living in a Dangerous Society

It is difficult to prove that the United States has actually become a more dangerous place for children than it was at any time in the past. Certainly children are more protected now from industrial accidents than they were before child labor laws were passed. Improved medical care and advancements in medical science mean that fewer children die from life-threatening diseases.

But there are pervasive threats to children today. In some communities, children are at risk because of criminal violence that spills over and hurts innocent victims as well as the intended targets. James Garbarino, the director of the Erickson Institute, compares some inner-city communities to war zones and finds that children are similarly affected in both environments. In his own city of Chicago, the rate of serious assault increased 400 percent from 1974 to 1991 (1992, ix). Crime, however, is not the only source of danger for contemporary children. Some are at risk from violence inflicted on them by their own parents. Others live in environments that are life-threatening because of air pollution, toxic waste, or uncontrolled street traffic.

Garbarino's work with children in dangerously violent situations has convinced him that there are two significant dimensions of danger. One is objective, the actual likelihood that an individual may suffer harm or injury because of a particular situation. The other dimension is subjective, the apprehension that harm is imminent, a feeling of impending danger (p. 4). This subjective feeling of anxiety or fear can also be traumatizing to children. Children's healthy physical, social, and emotional development depends on their feeling secure enough at home and in their neighborhood to explore, play, and form relationships with other children and adults. They must feel safe in school in order to learn. Children who feel safe are more likely to grow up to be confident, competent adults than those who constantly worry about impending danger. In other words, even the perception of danger can be damaging to a child.

There is evidence that many children do worry about impending dangers of all kinds. Gene Del Vecchio (1997), an expert in marketing products to children, observes that children today are more aware of the adult world than children were in the past. Their sources of knowledge include both adult and children's news media; they also acquire a great deal of misinformation, rumor, and false knowledge from their peers. Del Vecchio quotes a 1996 Roper Youth Report that rank-ordered the concerns of children as follows: AIDS, kidnapping, drugs, homelessness, neighborhood crime, racial discrimination, pollution, divorce, nuclear war, having to fight a war, and the amount of TV violence (p. 129). *Newsweek* recently reported that 80 percent of our country's ten- to twelve-year-old boys and girls want to know more about being safe from violence; 73 percent want to learn more about AIDS (Kantrowitz and Wingert 1999, 67).

At least some of children's fears are justified. Teenagers, for example, who account for only 14 percent of the population age twelve and over, are the victims of 30 percent of all violent crime. In 1991, one of every ten 19-year-olds had been a victim of a violent crime. Twenty-five percent of all violent crimes against young people occur at home; 23 percent at school (Sanders and Mattson 1998, 140-41). More than 20 percent of all American middle schools and high schools reported at least one serious crime such as rape or robbery in the 1996-1997 school year. On the other hand, more than 43 percent of all public schools reported no crimes at all. Still, if children do not feel safe at home and at school, where can they feel secure?

The rash of well-publicized shootings on school campuses in 1998 and 1999 has generated a lot of fear about the safety in the institution in which children traditionally spend most of their daytime hours. In January 1999, 27 percent of teenage boys and 19 percent of girls listed violence as the biggest issue facing their generation. In May, following the shootings in Littleton, 51 percent of the boys and 56 percent of the girls ranked it first (Goff 1999, 53). Parents in Florida who chose to homeschool their children cited safety as the number one reason they pulled their children out of public schools (Kantrowitz and Wingert 1998, 66).

Whether justified or not, many parents perceive the world as being a more dangerous place for children than it was when they were young. One mother quoted in *Newsweek*'s 1999 survey article on children yearned for the lost innocence of her own childhood, "when we could play in the woods for hours by ourselves and our parents had no reason to worry." She believes that she has to be much more protective of her own nine-year-old daughter. "You have no choice but to tell them about things like sexual predators and kidnappers," she said (Kantrowitz and Wingert 1999, 68).

A ten-year qualitative sociological study of preadolescent children in grades three to six in a middle-class town noted that the fear of children being unsupervised in public space was one of two reasons for the increase in organized after-school activities. The other reason was the increased number of working mothers (Adler and Adler 1998). Gavin de Becker (1999) has written a book that offers parents techniques for protecting their children from personal violence, with advice about hiring babysitters, ensuring safety at school, helping teenage girls deal with boys, guarding against pedophiles, and the many other issues that frighten parents. Even de Becker, however, notes that the threats parents worry about the most—kidnapping and molestation by strangers—are statistically very unlikely to occur.

Growing up in a society that is perceived as dangerous has significant consequences for children. As noted, many children are actually at risk from violence of various kinds. Others are so protected from the possibility of danger that they are unable to explore their social worlds in ways that promote healthy development.

One could argue that young people who perpetrate violence are also victims of the society in which they live, so bombarded by violent images and events that they are either traumatized or benumbed by it. However, fewer politicians and judicial authorities are accepting the argument that children cannot be held fully accountable for their violent actions. Increasingly, the justice system is treating youthful offenders as though they were adults. After the first widely publicized schoolyard killings in Arkansas in 1998, states began enacting tougher penalties for adolescent murderers. Nearly every state has lowered the age at which children can be tried as adults and expanded the categories of crimes for which children can be sentenced to adult prisons (Fritz and Krikorian 1998). Newspaper accounts of trials of eleven- and thirteen-year-old killers make it clear that rehabilitation is no longer the prevailing intent; rather, courts are focused on protecting society from youthful offenders (Bradsher 1999; Simon 1999).

Libraries are also affected by the heightened public awareness of danger to children. Some libraries in high crime areas report that children are not allowed to visit unattended because of concerns about potential danger on the street. There is even concern that violence may move from the streets into the library. Many libraries are paying for highly visible security officers to help both staff and patrons feel safe.

Changing Families

The statistics tell a fascinating story. In spite of the representations on television sitcoms and in nostalgic school readers, only 43 percent all children in 1940 lived in families with a father who worked full time and a mother who was a full-time homemaker. By 1990, less than 20 percent of all children lived in "traditional" families (U.S. Census Bureau 1993, 2). Working mothers accounted for most of the change. Between 1980 and 1990, the percentage of working mothers increased from 60 percent to 72 percent (U.S. Census Bureau 1993, 9). By 1990, 24 percent of all children lived with one parent; and the numbers are much higher for nonwhites. 63 percent of all African-American children and 35 percent of all Hispanic children lived with one parent (U.S. Census Bureau 1993, 4).

While many women work for self-fulfillment, the primary reason for the increase in the number of working mothers appears to be economic. There are more opportunities for women to work than there were in 1940, and the second income is necessary to provide a comfortable way of life for many families. An article in the *New York Times* (Uchitelle 1999) used U.S. Bureau of Labor Statistics figures to demonstrate that a typical married couple with one or two children and a middle-class income of $49,700—the statistical mean—had to work an average of 3,860 hours in 1997. This is a workload of more than two full-time jobs and a significant increase from the average of 3,236 hours in 1979. The increase in two-income families and the general prosperity in the country may account for the overall decrease in poverty rates reported by the U.S. Census Bureau in 1997.

Although the number and percent of families in poverty have declined, the poverty rate for people under eighteen years of age was 19.9 percent in 1997, much higher than the rate for adults (10.9 percent) and for people older than sixty-five (10.5 percent). Children represent 40 percent of the poor in this country, even though they are only 25 percent of the total population. Children under six who live with a single mother have a poverty rate of 59.1 percent— more than five times higher than that of children living in two-parent families (Dalaker and Naifeh 1998, vi). The Annie E. Casey Foundation (1999) estimates that 20 percent of all children live in poverty and that 9 percent live in extreme poverty, in families where the income is below 50 percent of the official poverty level. Demographers note a disturbing growth in the income disparity between children from wealthy families and those from poor families (Federal Interagency Forum on Child and Family Statistics 1999, iv).

The most vulnerable children of all are the homeless, and their numbers are rising. A recent study conducted by Ellen Bassuk (O'Connor 1999), a Harvard professor of psychiatry for the Better Homes Fund reported that more than 1 million children in America are homeless, a greater number than at any time in our nation's history except the Great Depression of the 1930s. Women and children are the fastest-growing homeless groups. Life on the streets is so unsettling and traumatizing that Bassuk estimates that a third of all homeless children exhibit emotional and mental disorders by the time they are 8. Their rate of sexual abuse is three times higher than that of other children, and a quarter of them have witnessed family violence. Their intermittent school attendance at as many as three or four different schools in a single year hinders their academic performance and leads to social isolation. They are twice as likely as other children to be required to repeat a grade.

The most obvious consequence for children living in families where both parents work is child care or, in many cases, the lack of child care. Recent federal legislation requiring most adult welfare recipients to work has put an additional strain on an already inadequate child care system. The Children's Defense Fund (1999a) estimates that 65 percent of women with children younger than six and 78 percent of women with children between the ages of six and 17 work. Three out of five preschoolers—more than 13 million children—are in some kind of child care arrangement. Many school-age children have no day care arrangements at all; more than five million children are home alone after school every day.

The cost of child care is very high. According to the Children's Defense Fund, full-day child care typically costs from $4,000 to $10,000 a year, well beyond the reach of the one out of three families with young children whose income is less than $25,000 a year (1999b, 8). As a result, many parents patch together makeshift child care arrangements or settle for care that is less than desirable. A 1995 national study found that six out of seven child care centers offered care that was mediocre to poor, and one in eight were actually dangerous (Children Now 1998).

Quality child care for preschool children offers many of the benefits of good early childhood education programs. In addition to offering a safe, nurturing environment, children in good child care centers receive many early learning experiences that help them get ready to read and do well in school. In its 1999 overview report, the Children's Defense Fund summarizes a number of national studies that show, not surprisingly, that the benefits of quality day care are particularly significant for low-income children from diverse backgrounds. Children who received high-quality child care during their preschool years scored higher in their ability to use and understand language and in their mathematical ability than children who were in poor-quality child care arrangements. They also showed greater thinking and attention skills and had fewer behavior problems in their early elementary years. They were even more likely to attend a four-year college and to delay parenthood (p. 5). Many policy experts calculate that an investment in good child care for preschool children actually saves money that would otherwise be spent on special education, welfare, and criminal justice programs.

School-age children also benefit from quality after-school programs. Studies have shown that they got along better with their peers, were more emotionally stable, did better in school, and spent less time watching television than children who were unsupervised after school (Children's Defense Fund 1999b, 5). One three-year study of children living in high-crime neighborhoods found that those who attended after-school programs developed better work habits and conflict management skills than those who did not. Unfortunately, fewer than 33 percent of the schools in low-income communities offer after-school programs, compared with 40 percent of schools in more-affluent neighborhoods (Children's Defense Fund 2000).

The lack of adequate, affordable child care for working parents has had a major impact on public libraries. Many have become de facto after-school child care centers. Los Angeles County Public Library has been tracking the number of latchkey children in its libraries after school since 1985, basing its statistics on a count during one typical week during the year. In June 1985, libraries reported a total of 1,456 latchkey children using their facilities, of which 292 appeared to be "full time"; that is, visiting the library unattended four or five times a week. By June 1999, the number of latchkey kids had increased to 5,081, with more than half of them full time. The youth services coordinator for the library noted that in most cases staff coped well with the situation by instituting strict standards of behavior, seeking community support, and developing more after-school programs. Homework centers have been established in twenty branches. Still, 27 percent of the staff found the latchkey children to be a problem (Markey 1999).

Some public libraries have been so burdened by latchkey kids that they adopted "unattended children" policies. The libraries in San Marino, South Pasadena, and Long Beach, California, all deny access to children under ten or eleven who are unaccompanied by adults. These are libraries in large metropolitan areas where you might expect administrators to be particularly wary of potential dangers to children on their own. But even small-town libraries, like the one in Indiana's Bloomfield-Eastern Green County, serving 2,500 people, have found it necessary to restrict access by unattended minors (Winton 1999).

In addition to the changes in family structure noted by the U.S. Census Bureau, other social trends are affecting children's lives. Increasing numbers of lesbian and gay parents are raising children—adopted children, offspring from earlier heterosexual marriages, or the products of birth technologies such as artificial insemination and in vitro fertilization. Surrogate mothers who serve as the birth mother for another woman's child have given new hope to couples who have been unable to bring a pregnancy to term and have ignited some heartbreaking legal battles as well. The Census Bureau also reports that the number of grandparents who are rearing their children's children is on the rise. In fact, one in every twenty children in the United States lives in a home headed by his or her grandparents. Sociologists attribute the increase in what they call "skipped generation" arrangements to a range of factors, from drug use and divorce to incarceration and AIDS-related deaths (Fuzesi 1999).

The last issue affecting the lives of children in America today is complex and contentious. It is the matter of children's rights.

The Tension over Children's Rights

People who want to ensure that children are protected from abuses of all kinds and people who want to expand children's autonomy both use the rhetoric of children's rights, although they are usually on different sides of policy issues. One scholar sees the controversy over children's rights as a tension between two competing concerns about their welfare: protecting children from their own mistakes, even if it means limiting their choices and behavior, versus giving children more freedom and autonomy, even if it means risking the possibility of their making some bad choices. She explains, "Protectionists emphasize that children have a right to assistance and care from adults, whereas liberationists emphasize that children have a right to self-determination" (Ladd 1996, 2).

From a legal perspective, it is children's dependency or presumed lack of competence that often prevents their being granted the rights of adults. Interestingly, the same arguments were made to deprive American women of their rights until the twentieth century. One prominent legal scholar has noted the double dependency of children, who in American society have been entrusted to the care of their parents. They are dependent in the eyes of the law and by the actual circumstances of their lives. "Children's dependencies," she writes, "specifically situate them within the sphere of the private family, where parents stand between children and state" (Minow 1996, 52). It is understandable that in this legal framework children's rights focus on such protectionist issues as the right to be free from abuse and neglect.

Laurence D. Houlgate (1980, 22ff.) points out that because children are legally in the custody of their parents, who are responsible for supervising them and taking care of their general needs, young people have few legal rights of liberty at home. Parents have the right to decide where their children will live, what they will eat, how they will dress, and what they will read. The state determines that a child must attend school until a minimum age (usually sixteen), and parents are responsible for enforcing that requirement. Parents are legally responsible for the consequences of their children's behavior in many cases, whether that means replacing a neighbor's window shattered by a child's ball or paying for a lost library book.

This assumption of parental responsibility for children's behavior underlies the requirement in most public libraries that a parent cosign for a child's library card. Sometimes an additional signature is required before a child can check out videos and other items that may incur significant financial penalties if they are lost or returned late. The requirement of an additional signature may also give parents the implicit right to restrict their children's access to R-rated videos.

Libraries have resisted efforts to act in loco parentis, that is, to take responsibility for children's information-seeking behavior. Local libraries and the American Library Association have repeatedly refused to enact policies that limit children's access to specific materials other than for financial reasons as in the case of the aforementioned video policies. Their refusal stems partly from the profession's long-standing tradition of protecting individuals' First Amendment rights. But the more compelling reason is that librarians do not want to be put in the position of determining what information is appropriate for a person's children. Librarians have overwhelmingly come to say, both in official policies and in their transactions at reference desks, that it is the responsibility of parents to determine what their children read.

This pragmatic policy has stood public librarians well through many censorship controversies. It has the appeal of common sense. It makes it possible for the librarian to be supportive of a specific parent's concern about what a child might be reading without actually removing the questioned book from the shelves. It also makes it possible for libraries to respond to the cultural diversity and range of ideologies in their communities without catering to the demands of any one group or powerful individual.

In practice, no one questions the vast majority of materials that are typically available to children in public libraries. Although most children's librarians have encountered at least one challenge in their careers, perhaps a concern about witchcraft in a folktale or the portrayal of African Americans in a book about slavery, they have been able to respond within the rubric of accepted professional practice, citing both their collection development policies and the library's recognition of the responsibility of parents to monitor their own children's reading. As noted in chapter 3, however, the availability of much more controversial material on the Internet has made the librarians' position less tenable. Children's librarians might disagree about the actual harm done to a child by viewing pornography or hate speech on the Internet, but few would actually advocate that the library make such materials available to children. Few librarians would recommend that they add misleading or inaccurate information to their collections, but software filtering doesn't take care of this problem at all.

As noted earlier, some members of the public and elected officials are increasingly calling on public libraries to protect children from viewing materials that are considered harmful. More and more libraries are putting filters on computers that are available to children, in spite of librarians' reservations about the effectiveness of this approach and their concerns about the useful information that is filtered out along with the bad.

I have suggested elsewhere (Walter 1997) that children's librarians have a responsibility to teach their patrons how to use the Internet effectively, and in the next chapter I will discuss some of the ways they are doing this. The American Library Association (ALA) also advocates taking an educational approach to Internet usage, while at the same time developing clear Internet use policies that make the limitations on the library's responsibilities to patrons very clear. One of the two key messages in ALA's publication *Libraries and the Internet Toolkit* is that "the best protection for children is to teach them to use technology properly and to make good choices" (2000, 1).

Jon Katz, a frequent contributor to *Wired,* suggests another approach to children's "cyber rights." He advances the notion of the responsible child and suggests that parents negotiate a new social contract with children who are approaching adolescence. If the children meet certain criteria, such as applying themselves diligently to schoolwork and household chores and following normal rules of age-appropriate conduct, they can be considered responsible for their own decisions and be given some rights that are currently problematic for young people. These include the right to have access to their culture, to assemble on-line, to challenge the use of blocking software and other technologies that arbitrarily deny them choice, exposure to ideas, and freedom of speech (1996, 166).

While the issue of children's rights is an old one, the impetus to protect children seems to have become stronger as more and more adults have come to view the world as a dangerous place. The Internet has brought some of the perceived dangers from the streets right into libraries and private homes, where adults always assumed children were safe. Ironically, the increasing violence in our society has actually eroded some of the traditional protections for children, those that were institutionalized in the juvenile justice system. More young children accused of violent crimes are being tried as adults. This trend has less direct ramification for librarians working with children than the drive for Internet restrictions, but it is a telling example of our society's confusion about its children.

Although First Amendment issues are probably the most obvious arena for librarians' involvement with children's rights, privacy is another area of concern. Once again, social change has resulted in an unexpected consequence for children. The specific privacy issue that troubles children's librarians is the question of a parent's access to information about a child's library record. It is not unusual for a parent to ask to see a child's circulation record. Almost always, the parent is simply trying to make certain that the child's checked-out books have been returned; and almost always, the record would be made available for that reason.

The Contra Costa Public Library, however, determined that this policy compromises a child's right to privacy. The legal counsel for the library determined that a child has the same right to confidentiality at the library that an adult does, and parents in this county were no longer given this information when they asked. Now a child can check out materials about dealing with abusive parents, for example, without fear of discovery. The library also discovered that this policy helped ensure the safety of children in hotly contested custody cases where a noncustodial parent could use the ploy of checking a child's library record in an effort to obtain the child's current address (Hildebrand 1997).

Many librarians are parents themselves, and they know firsthand how changes in our society are affecting their children. They try to make wise decisions about introducing them to rapidly evolving information technology. They want their children to get a good education. They rejoice at the increasing diversity of their society and worry about the harm caused by racism and poverty. They worry about how to protect their children in what seems to be an increasingly violent society, and then worry that they are worrying too much. They cope with changing family structures of their own and search for good child care arrangements. They must thread their way through the tangle of children's rights at home as well as at work.

Whether they are parents or not, children's librarians are advocates for the best interests of all children. They monitor the changes in the lives of the children they serve and try to adapt their services to meet new needs and new situations. In the next chapter, I will look at emerging trends in public libraries that may suggest patterns for effective library services for future kids.

CHAPTER

5

Emerging Trends in Library Services for Children

ALTHOUGH THE TRADITIONAL SERVICES described in chapter 2 still comprise the heart of most public library programs for children, there are new approaches and trends that may signal significant shifts in direction. These trends include Internet access and patron training, homework assistance, service to homeschoolers, service to infants and toddlers, and services for parents. Many of them have their roots in earlier children's services, yet they all represent new priorities, new competencies for staff, new practices, and perhaps a new ideology. These new trends in library service to children are interrelated, but I will discuss each of them separately.

Internet Access and Training

One significant social development that affects children's lives today, discussed in chapter 4, is the emergence of digital information and communication technology. Once the special toy of academics and computer geeks, the Internet has captured the attention of everyone from policy makers, pornographers, and entrepreneurs to soccer moms, day traders, and elementary school children. Nearly three-quarters of all public libraries are now wired to offer Internet access to the public.

In this time of rapid expansion of digital technologies, public services staff in many libraries are finding that it is not enough to install public access computers. They have to teach people how to use this new tool to access information effectively.

People assume that children use new information technologies more readily than adults do. Children, after all, are not afraid of the computer. Yet many researchers have found that although most children do indeed approach computers more confidently than adults do, they do not necessarily use them effectively for information retrieval. The ubiquitous on-line library catalog is a good example. One interesting study done when many school and public libraries were converting from manual to on-line catalogs showed that some children had devised effective, if unconventional, strategies for finding materials in a printed card catalog. Persistence was sometimes rewarded; they could, for example, just keep thumbing through the cards until they found something that looked good (Edmonds et al. 1990). On-line catalogs don't provide the same opportunity for browsing, and spelling errors can sabotage an otherwise sound search.

A four-year study conducted at the University of California at Los Angeles (UCLA) compared the performance of children using traditional electronic library catalogs to those using an experimental Science Library Catalog designed by the project team. The Science Library Catalog, which ran on low-end Macintosh computers, featured a graphical interface to the Dewey-based hierarchy of classification numbers using a visual bookshelf metaphor. This was intended to correspond to children's mental model of a library catalog. Children did, in fact, find it easy to browse the experimental catalog by moving through successive levels of the classification hierarchy that was represented by images of cascading bookshelves.

Among the interesting findings from the UCLA study was that children tended to abandon searches in traditional on-line catalogs more readily than in the open-ended Science Library Catalog. If their searches were unsuccessful in conventional on-line catalogs, they often assumed that the library had no books on those topics. It did not occur to them that their search strategy might be ineffective. Poor keyboarding and spelling skills, a limited vocabulary, and difficulty in formulating Boolean searches all make it difficult for children to use most electronic library catalogs. It is not surprising, then, that most children would rather not use a catalog as a finding tool at all. Their first choice in locating a book is to browse the shelves where they have found books in the past; their second choice is to ask a librarian for help (Borgman et al. 1995; Walter et al. 1996). In her continuing work with the Science Library Catalog, Sandra Hirsh (1997) confirmed that the complexity of the search task and the amount of knowledge a child has about a topic also affect his or her ability to find information in a catalog.

The skills needed to find information in a text-based on-line library catalog might be difficult for some children to master, but at least they are concrete. They are definable skills that adults can pass on to children. The World Wide Web presents a whole new set of skills for children to learn, including the more broadly defined competencies assumed under the rubric of information literacy.

A simple definition of information literacy is the ability to access, evaluate, and use information from a variety of sources. An information literate person:

recognizes that accurate and complete information is the basis
 for intelligent decision making

recognizes the need for information

formulates questions based on information needs

identifies potential sources of information

develops successful search strategies

accesses sources of information, including computer-based and
 other technologies

evaluates information

organizes information for practical application

integrates new information into an existing body of knowledge

uses information in critical thinking and problem solving
 (Doyle 1994, 3)

Obviously, information literacy is an inclusive term that incorporates many elements of critical thinking, problem solving, and research. Most public librarians would not feel qualified to teach the entire package to their library patrons, who are not the "captive audience" that school children are. Not surprisingly, school library media specialists and university librarians have developed the most inclusive approaches to teaching information literacy. The 1998 edition of *Information Power*, prepared by the American Association of School Librarians and the Association for Educational Communications and Technology, presents nine standards for student learning in the area of information literacy and suggests ways that school library media specialists and teachers can work together to incorporate information literacy into the curriculum.

Some public librarians are beginning to take responsibility for educating their patrons in the higher skills associated with information literacy. Charles Curran (1990) points out that there is nothing new about the concepts associated with information literacy. What is new is the abundance of information that is available, the variety of formats in which it exists, and its importance to people's lives. Public librarians find they must adopt a more educational role in order to guide people to the wealth of information in cyberspace.

Some libraries successfully counter the pressure to use filtering software by giving children a basic foundation in information literacy and guidance in using the World Wide Web. By offering Internet classes to the public, a library signals its willingness to take some responsibility for teaching children to use the Web safely and effectively (Walter 1997). There are several innovative models for teaching children and parents how to use the World Wide Web and other digital resources. Most incorporate basic elements of information literacy. Let's look at a few of them.

Since the mid-1990s, at-risk children in Baltimore have been introduced to the World Wide Web through the Whole New World program, an eight-week session that gives young people the confidence and the competence to use e-mail, chat, library catalogs, and the World Wide Web. When they complete their training, with the help of trained volunteers, they are "licensed to drive" (Mondowney 1996).

Carroll Davey, a children's librarian in Jefferson County, Colorado, developed a more streamlined one-session introduction to Internet safety and search strategies for children and parents. In a program presented at the Association for Library Services to Children's 1998 annual conference Davey showed how she distilled this complex topic down to basic and comprehensible guidelines that could be absorbed in one sitting.

In 1999, the Santa Monica Public Library created a position for a digital resources children's librarian who guides the library's policies and practices for children in the digital arena. The main library has a computer training room where the digital resources children's librarian offers Internet classes for children and parents.

The San Francisco Public Library (SFPL) has a well-endowed Electronic Discovery Center in its main children's room and six branches, with plans to expand to all twenty-six branches. With major funding from the National Science Foundation Digital Library project and many corporate and community partners, the center has incorporated a number of training elements into its service operation. Volunteers are trained to work one on one with children in the Electronic Discovery Center, and short introductory classes are offered to parents. Weeklong summer institutes train teachers and school librarians to use the library's electronic resources (SFPL 1999).

Another project that targets parents is ParenTech, the result of a partnership between Ameritech, the North Central Regional Educational Laboratory, and the Association for Library Service to Children. The ParenTech kit, distributed to schools and libraries, includes three parent guides, an interactive CD-ROM, and a Web site (www.parentech.org). These resources introduce parents of middle-school children to current issues involving technology and suggest activities that highlight the educational potential of digital media. The kit gives parents a good foundation for guiding their children to the most effective uses of the new information technologies.

Homework Assistance

Public libraries have always been a resource for homework assignments, but only recently have they begun offering formal homework assistance. In his introduction to a forum on public libraries and homework help that was published in *Public Libraries*, Don Sager (1997) noted that helping students with homework had become so common in public libraries that it blended into the woodwork. There have been times in the recent past, however, when public libraries rejected homework help as one of its responsibilities or felt overwhelmed by the prospect of trying to meet student demands. In 1961, Los Angeles Public Library Director Harold Hamill applauded the tightening of academic standards that had resulted in an increase in students' need for library materials. "The problem is that our public libraries are not equipped to handle this increasing trend," he added. (Moore 1961, 220).

In a growing number of libraries, however, homework assistance has become a formal service initiative. With a Fyan research grant from ALA, Cindy Mediavilla (1999) has been studying homework centers throughout the United States. She notes two different motivations for establishing formal public library homework centers. Libraries are either responding to the after-school inundation of younger latchkey children or to an identified need of teenagers for something beyond reference service. She has discovered many examples of library homework assistance programs, with varying levels of funding. What they all require, however, is a commitment from the community they serve. Partnerships with local organizations, businesses, and schools contribute to the success of the homework centers by providing resources and support (Mediavilla 1998).

Robert Reagan (1997) reports that Los Angeles Public Library's homework centers are a response to a broad range of challenges the library has been facing. These include keeping kids interested in libraries after they leave elementary school, attracting new sources of funding, keeping up with advances in electronic technology, and keeping the support of elected officials. The computer-based homework centers provide a wide range of software for students of all ages. Tutors help with using the computers but do not actually help with homework.

Some libraries do offer formal tutoring as part of their homework center services. Among these are the PASS! program at the Oakland Public Library in California; Homework Helper centers in Minneapolis, Minnesota; the Latchkey Enrichment program at Queens Borough Public Library in New York; and the Homework Tutoring program at the St. Joseph County Public Library in Indiana (Machado et al. 2000). All of these programs use paid or volunteer aides who work directly with young students in the library.

The Toledo-Lucas County Public Library in Ohio also staffs its homework centers during the after-school hours with paid staff and trained high-school volunteers. Funding from Conrail enabled the library to buy CD-ROM encyclopedias, textbooks, and school supplies such as rulers, staplers, and glue sticks (Clark 1997).

In the small suburban community of Westwood, Massachusetts, the library addresses the homework needs of its students through systematic cooperation and collaboration with its schools. The library makes it clear that it intends only to supplement the work of school libraries, which still have the primary responsibility for curriculum support (Viti 1997).

A very effective example of cooperation between schools and public libraries is the Tall Tree Initiative in Westchester County, New York. Funding from the DeWitt Wallace-Reader's Digest Fund is intended to encourage staff to rethink what schools and libraries can do for young people. Pat Tarin, a consultant for the program, articulated the vision for the two institutional partners: "Think of yourselves as a single support system for the student, not as two separate entities" (Rockfield 1998, 31). The schools and public libraries make an effort to plan cooperative activities that help children connect what they're learning at school to the public library and vice versa. Their programs include a young authors program, an annual exposition at which students present their new information skills to the community, a book club, a club devoted to science and math books, a courier service between a school and its public library, and a homework hot line voice mail system.

What all of these homework assistance programs have in common is a willingness on the part of the public libraries to take on a broader educational role and to relax the boundaries between the mission of the public library and that of the school library. Even in communities where school libraries are well funded, they are rarely open in the evening or on weekends, the times when children are most likely to need them for homework support. Librarians acknowledge that homework represents an important information need for children, and many are taking creative steps to meet that need through homework assistance programs.

Service to Homeschoolers

One of the changing circumstances in the lives of children that was discussed in chapter 4 is the increasing number of children who are being educated at home. A few parents who choose to educate their children themselves deliberately avoid contact with all secular or government institutions, including libraries. Many, however, rely heavily on the resources of their local public libraries. A survey in one county in the state of Washington showed that 93 percent of the homeschoolers there used the public library as a resource, with 54 percent visiting the library on a weekly basis.

Susan Madden (1997) noted the concerns these homeschoolers sometimes raise in the libraries they use, along with some solutions. Libraries worry about censorship pressures because many homeschooling parents from fundamentalist religious traditions feel strongly about limiting their children's access to subjects such as the occult or evolution. In response, Madden suggests that librarians develop good working relations with local homeschool groups so they will have a forum for explaining the library's perspective. She notes that homeschooling parents ordinarily accompany their children to the library. They are eager to exercise their parental rights to control their children's reading, so the library is usually not called upon to act *in loco parentis.* The other challenges that homeschoolers present to libraries are related to their heavy usage. Libraries worry that this one small group demands too much service or places too big a demand on the collection or the computers. Madden suggests homeschooled children be treated like all other students and homeschooling parents like all other educators. This should ease concerns about equity.

In some cases, libraries have been proactive about providing services to homeschooling families. Multnomah County offers workshops on Internet resources to homeschool groups. The King County Library in Washington State, where many homeschoolers live, has prepared information packets that contain a summary of local homeschooling law, book lists, and outlines of library services. The library also participates in the annual state homeschooling convention. Another library in Pennsylvania offered an opportunity for one nine-year-old homeschool child to conduct preschool story hours as part of her own learning experience (Avner 1997).

Susan Scheps (1999) notes a number of trends in the homeschooling movement. She finds that more parents are educating their children at home because of dissatisfaction with the public schools or a desire for family closeness rather than for religious reasons. More parents are creating their own curricula rather than relying on packaged course work. Mainstream publishers, as well as the small Christian firms that once dominated this field, are producing materials for homeschoolers. The Internet has been a revolutionary vehicle for helping to create nationwide networks of homeschoolers and for providing educational resources on-line. Scheps points out that libraries are uniquely able to help with a homeschooler's basic resource needs, such as information on one topic at various reading levels so that children of different ages can work on same project.

While aggressive homeschooling parents can sometimes threaten to overwhelm a small public library with their intense demands for resources and services, they can also be effective advocates for the library during budget hearings. One homeschooling mother offered this testimonial to the public library: "It offers a wealth of choices, a community that shares passion for reading and learning, and a place where each of us is respected for our interests without judgment" (Boone 2000, 11). Many children's librarians also find that serving homeschoolers is very satisfying. Providing the kind of individualized service these parents want comes easily to librarians who have been socialized in the tradition of providing the right book for the right child at the right time.

Service to Infants and Toddlers

As noted earlier, public libraries have been offering preschool story hours since the mid-1950s. The national emphasis on early childhood programs such as Head Start gave the story hour a boost in the 1960s, and now nearly all public libraries offer it in some form. These short programs—few were actually an hour long—were originally intended for three- and four-year-old children who were developmentally ready for a group experience.

The preschool story hour was designed to provide an early peer experience; to expose children to books and literary language; and to give them skills in listening, sitting still, and concentrating that would help prepare them for school. Parents were usually excluded, and if their child wasn't ready for the separation, they were told to try again when the child was a little older.

The preschool story hours featured early childhood classics such as Wanda Gag's *Millions of Cats* (1928), *Whistle for Willie* by Ezra Jack Keats (1964), or the more recent standard, Bill Martin Jr.'s *Brown Bear, Brown Bear: What Do You See?* (1992). Librarians chose stories with a strong narrative line; rhythmic, repetitive text; pictures that would carry to a group of children; and plots and characters that appealed to young children. They sprinkled finger plays and nursery songs throughout the storytelling program to break up the pacing and involve the children. Some used flannelboard figures or puppets to vary the presentation technique.

In some cases, librarians began offering story times for the little brothers and sisters of their preschool clientele because the parents wanted them to be included, but the main impetus to provide programs for infants and toddlers was a growing awareness of the concept of emergent literacy, the notion that literacy was not a skill that one learned all of a sudden in first grade.

William Teale (1995) spelled out for librarians the ways in which the new research on emergent literacy changed educators' understanding of reading and writing development in childhood. It is now believed that learning to read and write begins ideally in infancy for children in a literate society. Experts tell us that reading, writing, and speaking skills develop concurrently and that learning to read involves a broad range of skills and knowledge, including a knowledge of stories, an understanding of the conventions of print, letter recognition, and phonemic awareness. Teale urged librarians to work with other family literacy programs in their communities and to offer their own story programs for children and parents both in the library and in other settings such as child care centers and clinics.

It is not uncommon now to find public libraries offering different story times for infants, toddlers, and older preschool children. These separate story times allow librarians to tailor their approach to the developmental ages of their young participants. Those who provide services for very young children must be aware of these developmental differences and respond with age-appropriate programming. Many librarians are adopting the developmentally appropriate practices advocated by the National Association for the Education of Young Children (Bredekamp 1987). Quality service for infants and toddlers even requires rethinking the physical environment in many libraries.

Sandra Feinberg, Joan F. Kuchner, and Sari Feldman (1998) remind librarians that very young children don't have the life experience or the cognitive ability to readily understand traditional rules for good library behavior. Librarians can help toddlers approach the library setting comfortably by ensuring that the equipment and furniture are toddler-size and designed to facilitate their ways of interacting with their world. Safe structures and partial walls help to define areas that have different functions and also allow children to explore. The open floor plans favored by many architects and library administrators may be too noisy when boisterous toddlers are involved with a successful story time.

Age-appropriate programming for infants and toddlers also requires new approaches. Many librarians find that children in this age group respond well to repetition and ritual, so they begin and end each story time with the same simple song or participation game. These children welcome what is familiar. Librarians also find that they use more songs and nursery rhymes and fewer, shorter stories with this age group. They have learned that toddlers' notoriously short attention span and need for physical activity can create some very unconventional audience responses. Finally, like all good early childhood service providers, they involve parents and caregivers actively in their programs for infants and toddlers.

Feinberg, Kuchner, and Feldman summarize the elements of good practice in early childhood services. Good practice:

is individualized, varied, cognitively and developmentally appropriate

provides equitable access to a rich array of resources and learning opportunities

reflects the strengths, interests, diversity, and needs of children and their family fosters continuous individual development and encourages creativity, critical thinking, cooperation, and problem-solving skills from birth into adulthood

implements appropriate policies, programs, and services

involves partnerships with parents, caregivers, and family service providers

is flexible, accessible, and responsive to children and families
(1998, 90)

To implement good practice as it is understood by early childhood professionals, library decision makers may have to rethink their approach to children's services. It is unreasonable to expect that the same professional would have the skills and the time to serve all children in a community, from infancy through adolescence, as is the case in many libraries. It is unreasonable to expect that the same facility or section of a building would be appropriate for children from infancy through elementary or middle school. It will be interesting to see if libraries begin to recognize the specialization of early childhood services by hiring librarians to work specifically with this age group. The library's credibility as a provider of early childhood services may well depend on this.

Service to Families/Parent Education

Increasingly, children's librarians are serving the whole family, not just the child. The new focus on infants and toddlers may have been the impetus. Obviously, babies don't come to libraries by themselves and don't leave their caregivers for the story hour. They need an adult lap to sit in.

Many parents do not have the information or the skills to share books, stories, and language activities with their very young children. As scientific evidence of the importance of early stimulation to children's subsequent cognitive development became common knowledge, libraries realized that they had an obligation to help parents in their critical role as their child's first reading teacher. The baby and toddler story time became an opportunity to model these skills for parents.

Many literacy coordinators in public libraries discovered that a primary motivation for many adults who enrolled in literacy programs was the desire to read to their children. They responded with family literacy programs that use children's books to teach parents how to read and family story times to model techniques for sharing books with children.

Sue McLeaf Nespecca reports that the best of these family literacy programs acknowledge the strengths, styles, and needs of individual families (1994, 10). Adults with poor literacy skills may feel uncomfortable in the library at first. They may worry about failing or being stigmatized. They may have different expectations about reading and books than more educated parents have. Many of the public library's services have evolved to suit the middle-class, educated people who are the institution's primary users. Librarians themselves are middle-class, educated people. It sometimes takes a leap of great empathy and resourcefulness to develop services that work for other groups.

Libraries for the Future, a national library advocacy organization, has joined forces with the Middle Country Public Library (N.Y.) and several funders to create a Family Place in library demonstration sites throughout the country. The intention is for the library to take the lead in promoting emergent literacy and healthy child development by supporting the efforts of parents. These libraries have thought about the physical facility and tried to make it family friendly. There are spaces to park strollers and comfortable chairs where parents and children can cuddle together with a good book. These libraries also conduct five-week parent-child workshops that combine library orientation, parent education, early intervention screening, parent support groups, and toddler play groups. The librarians collaborate with other agencies to provide information on topics such as nutrition or child development. Where needed, a bilingual librarian greets parents in Spanish (Feinberg and Rogoff 1998).

Another parent education program begun with outside funding is Read to Me L.A., a project of the Los Angeles Public Library. The major sponsor is GTE, a telecommunications firm, but it has additional support from the Riordan Foundation, the *Los Angeles Times*, the Ahmanson Foundation, Macy's West, and Rotary International District 5280. I list the sponsors because they are indicative of the trend away from reliance on local government budgets for innovative library programs. In Read to Me L.A., a project consultant or specialist from the children's services office trains volunteers who then give workshops to groups of parents on how and why to read to their preschool children. The training materials and the workshops are offered in Spanish and English.

I noted earlier in this chapter that some public libraries have also taken responsibility for teaching parents about the new digital technologies that are available for them and their children. Many adults have heard only the horror stories circulated in the media about Internet predators and pornographers. At the same time, they are eager for their children to reap the educational benefits of the Internet. The library's parent education efforts can be as modest as providing copies of *The Parents' Guide to Cyberspace*, an ALA publication, or as ambitious as holding a series of classes. By equipping parents with balanced, accurate information about the Internet, libraries do a great deal to establish themselves as credible and caring institutions.

What all of these emerging trends have in common is an expansion of the library's traditional function as a passive information provider to a more active educational role. Traditionally, public libraries have seen themselves as supplementing the work of schools in a fairly passive way, usually through the provision of books and information. Through these new initiatives, children's librarians in public libraries are taking a leadership role in some aspects of early childhood education and technology training. They have shown that they can be useful partners to parents who educate their children at home and to children who need homework assistance that their schools cannot provide. The public has responded favorably.

CHAPTER 6

Future Libraries and Future Kids

Some Alternative Visions

THE LAST DECADE OF THE TWENTIETH CENTURY was an ambiguous period in the chronicle of library services. Although the library profession, like other segments of society, was given to millennial reflection, it was often difficult for us to read the indicators and interpret their meanings. On the one hand, some social critics claimed that digital technologies would mean the end of libraries as we know them. On the other hand, many libraries were experiencing a renaissance of public support, as evidenced by bigger budgets and the building of lavish new central libraries across the country. Librarians were struggling to redefine their roles in the dot.com landscape. The more thoughtful among us admitted that our profession would continue to be faced with unprecedented opportunities and perplexing challenges.

We could go on as we have in the past. We have had an evolutionary history, adding slowly to our traditional services as new needs, opportunities, or resources presented themselves. But we haven't taken the time as a profession—or as individual practitioners—to rethink what libraries could do best for children growing up in the twenty-first century. This would be an excellent time for children's librarians to come forward with a coherent vision of library service for children, based on our core values and knowledge of children, society, and librarianship.

I suggest that we build our vision of future libraries for future kids as our foremothers did, those legendary women who designed public library services for children a hundred years ago. They started with a firmly held concept of the child as reader. As I look at the future, I see two additional concepts of the child that could inform our thinking—the child of the Information Age and the child in the community. Each of these three notions of the child leads to a different vision of library services. All three visions are plausible. All are hopeful. All are obtainable. They may not be mutually exclusive, but I have found it helpful to think about them separately. Each vision is based on a different understanding of the child who will claim and shape the twenty-first century.

The Child as Reader

The library for the child reader is the vision that offers the most continuity with the past. It builds on the core values and visions of the librarians who founded library services for children in this country. It aims to preserve the traditional niche that these services have occupied. It is thus a conservative vision, in the sense that it conserves a valued tradition.

The vision of a future library for the reading child contains several implicit assumptions. First, it assumes that books and reading will continue to be valued by our society. It assumes in particular that books and reading will continue to be essential to the healthy development of children. It also assumes that voters will agree that providing books and promoting reading for children are appropriate and even necessary functions for tax-supported public libraries. Note that these are normative assumptions—ideas about what the world should be. If we want to develop library services with the child as reader as the centerpiece of our efforts, we may need to hone our advocacy and marketing skills in order to keep books and reading as essential to taxpayers as they are to us.

Public libraries could tap into the current concern about children's reading. Most of the policy solutions that have been advanced so far to deal with the perceived crisis in children's reading focus on schools. Decision makers have looked for solutions in curriculum reform and the methods used to teach reading. Even with newer research that demonstrates the importance of early childhood experiences for the development of reading fluency in the primary grades, few policy makers have given attention to the role of public organizations in encouraging emergent literacy or in supporting to the reading curriculum in schools. The public library has wide acceptance as a book-oriented institution, but it still has a long way to go before proclaiming itself a major player in the childhood literacy arena.

But let's assume we have won that battle. What will future libraries for future child readers look like? These libraries will be informed by the latest research on emergent literacy, which tells us that reading children begin their exposure to language and literature as infants. They will contain separate, well-defined spaces that invite infants and toddlers and their caregivers to spend time with books. Little kids will find carpeted floors and safe, toddler-sized furniture. Parents and caregivers will find rocking chairs or comfortable sofas that are just right for intergenerational book sharing. I envision story time space right there with the books and other age-appropriate realia and separate rooms where the librarians will hold classes in children's literature, book-sharing techniques, and methods for encouraging emergent literacy for parents, child care providers, and other interested adults.

This library for the child reader of the future will have versatile shelving that will allow librarians to merchandise books as bookstores do, calling attention to multiple copies of inviting titles. There will also be traditional child-sized linear shelves for the basic collection that will make it easy for older children to negotiate their way through the library conventions of alphabetization and the Dewey decimal system. Child-friendly signs will give children visual and print pointers to different parts of the collection.

Future child readers will find spaces where they can curl up and be alone with a good book and spaces where they can talk about books with friends and library staff. They will find spaces for enjoying puppet shows, plays, and story-telling. They will find quiet, calm corners and noisy, stimulating areas. They might find a display of books about plants and gardening next to a window-ledge garden, an abacus placed next to books on math, and a table set up with a microscope, magnifying glass, periscope, and books about optics or science experiments. Everything in the library will communicate the impor-tance, the relevance, and the excitement of reading.

Obviously, the book collection will be the cornerstone of this vision of the future library. The carefully chosen book collection will be the base that sup-ports all other services. Children's librarians will have to hone their skills in book evaluation, collection development, and readers' advisory services to a razor's edge. Working from a deep understanding of their community, these librarians will seek out books that will enrich the lives of their young readers. They will work with editors, authors, and illustrators to encourage the devel-opment of new voices and new visions. They will see themselves as partners with publishing houses in marketing the best books for children. They will resolve the "quality versus demand" dilemma in ways that are consistent with the particular mission of their libraries, the needs of the children they serve, and the values of the communities in which they are located.

The reading-oriented library of the future will probably make judicious use of digital technologies. Certainly children need to be able to read in order to use the digital media available today, although voice recognition systems may be standard features on computers of the future. Even a library that emphasizes books and reading will need to concern itself with other forms of literacy in a world that increasingly values moving images as well as digital and visual media. As age-appropriate content develops for electronic books, children's librarians will surely want to make these available for their patrons.

Planners of the reading-oriented children's library will try to avoid the uneasy coexistence of print and digital resources that prevails in many libraries today. Children's librarians will carefully consider each technological innovation in light of their mission to encourage and enhance children's reading. Digital technology will not compete with books. Children will read the computer screen as well as the printed page and will learn when one format might be preferable to the other.

The librarians for young readers of the future will be passionate advocates for children's right to read, and their advocacy will take many forms. They will participate in traditional activities in defense of children's intellectual freedom. They will champion broad-ranging collection development policies based on sound book evaluation principles. They will also work to eliminate social, economic, and physical barriers to children's access to books and reading such as transportation difficulties or service hours that discriminate against working families. They will find ways to bring the resources of the library to children whose circumstances prevent them from coming to the library.

All of the services of this future library for reading kids will emphasize books and literacy. Readers' advisory and reference services will perhaps be the most important of public services. With their thorough knowledge of the collection, children's librarians will be recognized as skilled professionals who are best able to advise a child needing a good book for a school report, a parent seeking guidance about appropriate reading for a two-year-old, or a pediatrician looking for children's books on HIV/AIDS to share with a patient. They will extend their expertise through well-crafted book lists, bibliographies, and book talks.

Family literacy programs will fit well in the future library for the reading child. A library that places reading as its highest priority for children will cooperate with other like-minded community organizations and agencies, including schools. The library of the future could reasonably serve as the lead agency for any community-based literacy effort.

Programming at the reading-oriented library of the future will be consistent with its overall mission. Storytelling events, summer reading programs, and visits from authors or illustrators are obvious possibilities. Other programs might target smaller groups of children—book discussion groups, young writers' groups, poetry and science fiction clubs. Anything that promotes children's books and reading will be considered.

To implement this vision, we need to be as passionate and convincing as Anne Carroll Moore, Frances Clarke, and other library pioneers were. Libraries that clearly define their mission around the promotion of books and reading will find that this is a small but vital market niche they can occupy effectively.

There are possible pitfalls to a scenario that focuses on books and reading for children. Unless we are careful about how we craft the rhetoric of this vision, we could be marginalized or accused of nostalgia. We might appear stodgy and out of date to proponents of newer media, and to the children themselves. Certainly, an exclusive focus on reading leaves out whole areas of their lives that children care about very much.

The Child of the Information Age

A second image of the child that might inform our thinking about library services of the future is influenced by remarkable developments in digital technology. Many policy makers are fascinated by the possibilities for the child of the Information Age. Children today learn and play differently than they did ten or twenty years ago because of the power and seductiveness of the computer. In many cases, they also use libraries differently

Many librarians have observed that their public access computers draw children like magnets, especially boys. Young males who previously scorned the library as uncool or irrelevant now enjoy its CD-ROMs and Internet attractions. One boy who uses the Electronic Discovery Center at the San Francisco Public Library told an interviewer that although he had a computer at home, he liked the library computers better because he could meet his friends there and they could play on the computers together. I watched boys at the Chinatown Library in San Francisco play Dungeons and Dragons on two dumb terminals, completely engrossed in the fantasy world they were creating.

While they seem to prefer to explore the recreational functions of digital technology, these children of the Information Age also use computers for information when they must, usually for homework. We see children (and parents) in the library every day asking the librarian to "look it up in the computer, please." Most of our public libraries are now able to provide digital information resources for children. It might be a token computer in the children's room or a special facility with many Internet-capable computers in a new or renovated library. These machines often sit uneasily next to the bookshelves, though. Often, a volunteer or a young computer aide guides the children through the intricacies of computer access, while the children's librarian tends to their book-related needs.

What would it be like if we put digital technology first when we designed libraries for children of the Information Age?

Computers will take pride of place in the library for children of the Information Age. I can't say how many a particular library might need, but there will be enough so that waiting time will be minimal and libraries will not have to ration computer time as stringently as they do now. There might be one or two specially equipped computers that children can sign up to use, but the ordinary machines will be available on demand. The library will make a commitment to upgrade its computers as needed so they have the memory, operating systems, connectivity, and software to handle high-end computing tasks.

The computers in this library of the future will be placed in a variety of configurations throughout the children's room so they can be used by groups and individuals. Some machines will allow children to preserve their privacy while they access information. Some computers will feature a keyboard and mouse designed for very young children and will provide age-appropriate interfaces to software intended just for them. The computer desks, tables, carrels, and chairs will be ergonomically correct for children's use.

The library for children of the Information Age will include a well-equipped classroom where children, families, and concerned adults can learn the basics of information literacy. Librarians might conduct informal programs here to offer tips for Web searching and to share new Internet resources for kids.

Every computer in this future library will give children the option of using the regular catalog or one that is designed especially for kids. In either case, the catalog will point them to resources in all formats, including Web sites. When a child looks up "dinasor," for example, the catalog will correct the spelling and present a list of books, CD-ROMs, DVDs, magazine articles, and Web sites on the subject. A click on a book title might indicate the book's grade level and availability and then offer an animated map of the library that pinpoints that book's location on the shelf. A click on a magazine article might bring up the full text along with a word processing program that allows the child to take notes. A click on a CD-ROM will access the software; a click on a DVD, the movie; and a click on a Web site will bring it instantly to the child's screen. Impossibly futuristic? No, all of these features are possible now if we are willing to pay for them.

The current controversy about children's access to the Internet will be resolved by the time this future library is designed. Either government regulators will have brought the purveyors of hate and pornography under control or technologically superior filters will have truly eliminated what is illegal. Or perhaps children, parents, and elected officials will become so well educated in the skills of information literacy that nobody will worry about the possibility of a child stumbling onto an inappropriate Internet site.

We might have to enact policies that forbid adults who are unaccompanied by children from using the computers in the children's room. We wouldn't want grown-ups hogging machines that are intended for children or leaving their materials on the screen for children to find. Presumably there will be enough computers to satisfy adult needs in other sections of the library under this scenario.

Will there be books in the library for the child of the Information Age? Indeed, yes, as long as publishers continue to publish children's books that inform, entertain, and enlighten. There will certainly be electronic books for children, and the library will supply both the content and the readers for these. But there will also be a need for traditional printed books for years to come. As these future children become information literate, they will learn when it is best to use a digital resource and when a book is the best source for their information needs. Children's books will continue to be prized for their artistry, their ease of use, their tactile pleasures, and for the content that authors and illustrators created especially for that format. It is hard to imagine computers taking the place of a baby's first book or a child's bedtime reading.

Children's librarians in this scenario will be skilled Internet navigators, able to guide children and parents through the intricacies of Internet searching, safety, and etiquette. They will evaluate CD-ROMs and Web sites as knowledgeably as they evaluate picture books and novels. (Many children's librarians are already doing so. Just look at the 700+ Great Sites maintained by the Association for Library Service to Children and the American Library Association.) Above all, they will communicate to children the excitement and usefulness not only of books and reading, but also of digital media and information literacy.

The library for the child of the Information Age will undoubtedly employ other professionals in addition to children's librarians. These might include technicians who keep the equipment running, homework helpers who provide tutoring, and trained peer tutors who guide other children through cyberspace.

Without articulating this vision, many libraries are already leaning toward library service for children of the Information Age. It is a vision that plays well politically in many locations. Parents want their children to have the computer skills they need to succeed at school and in the workplace, and by and large they support the efforts of schools and libraries to provide computer resources. Although many adults worry about the well-publicized sexual predators and objectionable content that their children may encounter on the Internet, most still want their children to be computer literate.

Public libraries could occupy a unique social niche as a bridge over the digital divide. If we deployed sufficient resources into libraries in low-income communities, we could begin to close the gap between computer haves and have-nots. And if they take their mandate seriously—providing enough computers, relevant software, training, and convenient operating hours—public libraries could be the one place in the community where people of all ages can get meaningful access to the resources of cyberspace.

Although this vision of the public library is seductive, there are drawbacks to consider. Just as the previous scenario, the library for the child as reader, privileged books over digital resources, so this vision privileges digital media over print. And in the near future, when computers become as ubiquitous in the American home as televisions, the library's role in promoting equal access to digital resources will evaporate.

The public library could continue to play a role as technology leader, keeping one step ahead of the average home in its equipment and digital resources. This would be a very expensive proposition, of course, and there is little evidence that people would be willing to use their tax dollars for this purpose.

The library could maintain its function as a training center where people of all ages come to learn how to use the latest information technology. Expert librarians could give training classes for parents, provide tutorials for kids on using the Internet for various purposes, and advise day care providers on digital resources. To do this effectively, they themselves will need continual education and retraining.

A final deficit of the Information Age model for a children's library is that it offers little to the babies and toddlers who are such enthusiastic participants in traditional book and story-oriented events. These tiny patrons seem to benefit more from our story times and board books than from our computers. Some early childhood specialists admit that computers play a limited role in a well-rounded preschool program for children who are at least three years of age, but none is willing to claim that they have any benefits for babies and toddlers. The visionary pied piper of children's computing, Seymour Papert, cautions against using computers as "baby stimulators" or "baby-sitters," or using them to force learning at an artificially early age. He speculates that an infant's computer might take a very different form from the machines that currently sit on our desks. It might look like the stuffed objects that babies play with now. He writes, "The baby will use it by hitting it, touching it, gurgling or yelling at it, watching what it does and hearing the sounds it makes" (1996, 98). Now that I think about it, that's what my toddler grandchild does with her Teletubbie toy that has a microcomputer chip inside. It is primitive, but it is a computer, and she interacts with it just as Papert predicted.

The Child in the Community

My third vision for the future is a library for the child in the community. The child at the center of this vision is not primarily a reader or a computer user; this child is rooted in his or her community.

As children's lives have changed, so have the communities they live in. Many middle-class communities are ghost towns during the day as parents go off to work and children to school or day care. Other communities are held hostage to violence on their streets. Concerned parents keep their children inside, prisoners behind the security bars on the windows and doors. One family I know lives in a community where gang activity occasionally erupts in gunfire on otherwise peaceful streets. They have developed the habit of spending their time in the back rooms of the house, away from the path of stray bullets. The suburban housing developments where many families hope to escape the pathologies of urban life have turned out in many cases to be strangely isolated and alienating places with no center for people to congregate for bustling community-building activities.

The tragic schoolyard shootings of 1998 and 1999 forced many communities to look more closely at the environment in which their children are growing up. A parent in Littleton, Colorado, the affluent, suburban community that was the site of the shootings at Columbine High School, says, "We've become a garage-door society. We come into our homes with a click of a button. We close the door and our porches are in our backyards" (Cart 1999, A8). The wealthy southern California community of San Marino has zoning regulations that prevent children from playing in the front yard.

There are surely still places in this country where grown-ups sit on their porches or stoops and look after the children who play in their front yards and on the sidewalks. There must be communities where nosy neighbors can still be counted on to interfere when children misbehave or find themselves in trouble. General Colin Powell, who is the spokesperson for a national initiative to improve the lives of young people through volunteer efforts, talks about the informal network of "aunts" who supervised the block on which he was raised, watching out for the kids as they walked to school. He encourages communities to re-create these "aunt-nets" and to develop sanctuaries—safe places for kids to go after school (1998). Libraries could be those sanctuaries.

When Colin Powell reminisces about the neighborhood of his childhood, it is easy to dismiss his talk as nostalgia. It is not so easy to dismiss the reports of children themselves who talk about what's missing from their communities. A 1988 survey conducted by the Carnegie Foundation for the Advancement of Teaching found that only 59 percent of the fifth-graders and 45 percent of the eighth-graders reported that there were good places to play in their neighborhoods (Boyer 1991, 93). There is no reason to believe that anything has improved since then.

One recent study reported that the hours between 2:00 p.m. and 8:00 p.m., when many young adolescent and older children are neither in school nor under the supervision of their parents, account for more than 50 percent of all juvenile crimes. By the time they are twelve years old, nearly 35 percent of American kids are regularly left on their own (Alter 1998). We know that some of them show up as the ubiquitous, restless latchkey kids who present our public libraries with great challenges and opportunities. Other self-care children are home alone.

There are places where families can find rich offerings of after-school activities—music and dance lessons, youth organizations such as Girl Scouts and 4H. Many parents seek out additional educational opportunities for their children, from Hebrew lessons to tutoring in math. There is still a shortfall, however, between what is available and affordable and what families need.

Good communities for children would offer them rich, stimulating, safe environments in which they could explore the world outside their homes and families. There would be places to play and places to develop as unique individuals—arts and crafts centers, athletic facilities, parks, playgrounds, museums, and public libraries. There would be public spaces where children could have meaningful interactions with people from all generations. There would be opportunities to observe people at work and to participate in the life of the community, perhaps by serving on community youth councils, planning civic events, or volunteering to help other people.

The tradition of library services to children supports putting the child in the community at the center of our mission. The founders of library service to children spoke eloquently about the circumstances in which their young patrons lived. Since many of the earliest libraries to focus on children's services were urban, they often talked about crowded tenements and unsafe sweatshops where children labored for pennies. In a speech to the American Library Association in 1905, Frances Jenkins Olcott, head of the children's department of the Carnegie Library of Pittsburgh, talked about the demographics of Pittsburgh, where more than two-thirds of the total population of 321,616 were "either foreign born, or children of foreign born parents, and persons of negro descent" (p. 72). She was knowledgeable about the employment opportunities, the housing conditions, and the curriculum of the public schools. She knew her city inside and out, and she understood what living there was like for children.

Olcott noted that her children's department was reaching thousands of children through children's rooms in libraries and through the city schools. She worried, however, about the large numbers of children who didn't come into the library and were not enrolled in school. "These children work at home," she explained, "in toby shops, in factories, or they sell papers. There are also 'gangs' of restless boys who hang about street corners and whose lawless mischief leads them into crime" (p. 73). Olcott did not abandon these at-risk children. She organized an operation that cooperated with "institutions for social betterment," such as social settlements, the juvenile court, and the Newsboys' Home. The library staff established home libraries, small cases of books, in working-class homes. They would visit the homes, where they would gather a group of children and talk about the books, read aloud, tell stories, and teach crafts such as sewing or basketry. "The visitor from the library has a strong influence upon the home in which her group meets, as well as among the neighbors," Olcott explained. "She is often able to aid the families in case of illness, poverty, or lack of work, by putting them in touch with charitable institutions" (p. 74).

The children's department of the Carnegie Library of Pittsburgh also worked directly with boy gangs. Olcott discovered that these boys loved to read "trashy literature," even forming clubs that circulated the dime novels among themselves. To introduce the boys to more "improving" literature, she organized reading and game clubs, using clubrooms donated by school boards, mission houses, the Newsboys' Home, and a Jewish synagogue.

Olcott was a member in good standing of the sisterhood of early librarians who believed that the library had no higher purpose than putting fine literature in the hands of children. Yet she clearly understood that the children she was serving in Pittsburgh lived in particular communities, and she adapted her services to the circumstances of those children. I would submit that she designed her library services for the child in the community.

The outreach activities of the 1960s and 1970s again brought children's librarians out into the communities where their patrons—and potential patrons—lived. I remember telling stories in the playground of the housing project near the branch library where I worked in San Francisco in the late 1960s. It was eye opening to see how many children living just three blocks away had never found their way to the local library. In the early 1970s, I moved to southern California and worked for several years in the Boyle Heights barrio. My coworkers and I were tireless in our efforts to reach out to the Latino families in our neighborhood. We organized mothers clubs and community *posadas*. We told stories and sold *pinatas* at the *feria de los ninos* in the local park. We shopped at the local markets and ate lunch at Manuel's Burritos, home of the famous Hollenbeck burrito. One of my daughters went to camp with the local girls club, and my father helped the kids make a huge Frankenstein for the library's summer reading program. It was outreach based on person-to-person contacts as we tried to design library services for the children and families in our community.

That was then. This is now. How would we design library services for the child in the community today? We can't use a cookie-cutter approach because each community is different, but we can make some broad assumptions about what libraries might do for children in the community in the future.

Librarians designing services for children in the community will begin by getting to know the community very well, from a child's perspective. They will analyze the community systematically, gathering demographic data and information about the places, organizations, institutions, and people who are important in the lives of the children and families who live there. They will make personal contact with teachers, principals, storekeepers, day care providers, soccer coaches, religious leaders, PTA presidents, pediatricians, and others who interact with children. They will conduct interviews and focus groups with key individuals who can tell them what it is like to raise children or to be a child in that community. They will form cooperative relationships that can develop into partnerships for the good of the children.

After performing their initial analysis, librarians will monitor the community to detect shifts in the population and emerging issues of concern. They will know when crime is an issue and when parents are concerned about leadership in the schools. They will know where children can ride their bicycles safely and where they like to spend their allowances. By remaining active in the life of the community, librarians will not only acquire intimate knowledge of the children they serve; they will also establish their credibility and commitment.

Children's librarians will use the knowledge acquired from their ongoing environmental scans as the basis for the library services they provide. If their research shows that most school-age children are in home day care arrangements, they will look for ways to bring books and information services to those locations. If lack of day care is a problem, they will work with community leaders to find a solution and may offer to develop after-school programs at the library. If public meeting space is scarce, they will make the library's community room available to local organizations. If it has been difficult to recruit adult sponsors for youth groups, they may volunteer to lead one themselves.

Knowledge of the community will determine the library's service hours, the focus of the collection, and the ways in which technology is used. The library will also be a central resource for people to learn more about the community. Adults will look to the library for local information or referrals to sources of help. Kids might work with an adult staff member or volunteer to develop a database of helpful information—lists of good places to skateboard or play Frisbee, book and movie reviews, contacts for clubs and youth organizations, notices of special events. They might publish an electronic newsletter with similar information as well as samples of their own creative writing and editorials about topics of interest to kids.

The Public Library as a Mediating Institution

A public library that positions itself as a link between its users and the community in which they live is acting as a mediating structure. Sociologists have defined mediating structures as institutions that stand between individuals in their private lives and the large, impersonal organizations of public life (Berger and Neuhaus 1977, 2). Mediating structures are ordinarily small-scale, often informal, social organizations that help people negotiate their own needs and interests with large bureaucracies. Churches and voluntary associations are typical examples. Mediating structures are often incubators for incremental social change because they offer opportunities for people to develop grassroots organizing and leadership skills that they can use in the world at large (Evans and Boyte 1986). Cheryl Metoyer-Duran (1993) points out that key individuals also play mediating roles as gatekeepers in their own communities.

Too often, a public library might have been seen as one of those large, impersonal bureaucracies, alienating and cold, for which many people needed gatekeepers or mediating institutions in order to interact with it successfully. Children's librarians have sometimes seen themselves as the mediators between children's reading interests and information needs and the complex resources of the library. What I am suggesting here is something quite different—that the library itself help children to mediate between their private lives and the more public roles in their community.

If the library fulfills this mediating function successfully, it can facilitate access to the books and information children need to thrive. It can also nurture their overall development as productive members of society. When libraries see their young patrons as part of a community, they are likely to serve them holistically. I talked earlier about the DeWitt Wallace-Reader's Digest Foundation's efforts to help libraries function as partners in youth development. By encouraging young people to participate in the planning and implementation of services that affect them, libraries do a great deal to develop their civic awareness and sense of efficacy. Efficacy is the important belief that they can affect the world around them in positive ways. As children hit the "tween" years, from about ten to fourteen, it is particularly important that they see themselves as active participants in their communities. Libraries, through carefully designed and supervised programs of youth voluntarism and participation, can foster this growth.

In his introduction to a book on the importance of neighborhood organizations for young people John W. Gardner, former secretary of the U.S. Department of Health, Education, and Welfare, pointed out that it isn't enough for agencies to deliver specialized services to youth. They need to create environments in which young people can share a sense of responsibility and purpose and experience the benefits of building a community (McLaughlin, Irby, and Langman 1994, ix-xii). The authors of the book talk about how rare these environments are and how critical they are to children who are at risk of not reaching their potential. Libraries could help to create these urban sanctuaries for young people, within their walls and elsewhere in the community.

The Child in the Virtual Community

I have been talking primarily about the child in a physical community, where the library is a building that provides shelter in a sometimes hostile world, books and information to nourish the heart and mind, caring adults, and opportunities to grow. In that scenario, the library extends its arms into every corner of the community where a child might be—at home, school, the playground, the doctor's office, the day care center, gymnastics class, or soccer practice. The library can also offer a child entry into virtual communities.

Many observers have commented on the new virtual communities that have sprung up on the Internet. Howard Rheingold (1994), writing about the grassroots community building that is happening in cyberspace, calls it "homesteading on the electronic frontier." Sherry Turkle (1995) has written insightfully about the implications of virtual communities for redefining ourselves and taking on new roles in a world where nobody knows who we really are. While Internet role-playing and hanging out in chat rooms can lead children into an addictive and socially isolating fantasy world, it can also liberate those who have trouble with face-to-face communication to express themselves in new ways.

Dan Tapscott (1998) believes that young people who are immersed in the Internet culture are moving toward greater social inclusion. Their virtual interactions with people around the world foster a global perspective, he says.

He also describes situations in which communicating on-line has reduced the social isolation of deaf children and those who are considered different in their local community.

Librarians can leverage the benefits of virtual community building for children by guiding them to good experiences on-line. They can use their national and international professional contacts to establish on-line relationships between the children they serve, as individuals or in groups of keyboard pals. They can guide them to chat rooms and interactive Web sites that are monitored for safety, and they can help children create their own virtual community, with the library at the center.

Getting There

If children's librarians take their advocacy role seriously, they will start working now to create libraries that will serve the coming generations of children. The next chapter presents some strategies for getting there and getting it right.

CHAPTER 7

Getting It Right

IN THE PREVIOUS CHAPTER, I shared three scenarios for future libraries, each based on a different concept of the child. I outlined services libraries might offer if they targeted the child as reader, the child of the Information Age, or the child in the community as their primary user. The exercise demonstrated how different understandings of childhood in the future could inform our vision in different ways. We who care about children and libraries might not agree on one concept of childhood and one resulting pattern of services, but we should engage in a serious dialogue about the issues.

Children's librarians are practical people. We are very good at solving day-to-day problems. We can find the book about the old man with the ladder for a five-year-old reader who has forgotten everything else about this desired title. We can keep a rugful of toddlers busily engaged with stories for a reasonable length of time. We can tactfully divert the attention of an overbearing parent and help an anxious child find the book that's just right for her school report. We can disinfect headsets and teach a group of fifth graders how to play library quidditch. We can communicate effectively with library directors, elected officials, children's book editors, and preschoolers.

What we don't do so well, probably because we don't have time, is reflect on what we do and why we do it. As the first step to "getting it right" for the future, I urge all of us to reflect hard on what libraries can mean to tomorrow's children.

Step 1: Reflecting

Donald A. Schon (1983) called the kind of problem solving that children's librarians and other professionals do so well "thinking in action." At their best, professionals do more than just apply their technical knowledge to everyday problems of practice. They reflect on the limitations of the technical knowledge they bring to new problems, they reframe the problems, and they conduct informal experiments that may generate new ways of practice.

The innovation of toddler story times is a good example of children's librarians reflecting in action. Many librarians were taught that preschool story hours should be conducted as a first listening experience in a group setting without parents present. This was the conventional wisdom from at least the 1950s through the 1970s. As more mothers went to work in the 1980s, the preschool story hour audience shrank in many communities. Some librarians responded by shifting preschool story hour from the traditional morning time to early evening and inviting the whole family to participate. Librarians observed the value of including parents in their early childhood programs and found that little brothers and sisters could enjoy the story time experience if they didn't have to be separated from their parent or caregiver. After research underscored the importance of early childhood involvement with stories as a foundation for later reading success, librarians reframed their understanding of preschool story hours and positioned some of their story times as opportunities for parents to learn how to share books with their babies and toddlers.

What is required now is to extend the reflecting in action that good children's librarians do every day on the job to a more collective reflection. We need to begin a serious dialogue about what our profession and our institution should mean to children in the generations to come. We can begin the discourse in our own work organizations and then extend it to regional, state, and national associations. The process should be a consciousness raising for all of us as we try to clarify our values and our understanding of the work we do.

The end result of this should not be a homogeneous, one-dimensional vision of the future library for future kids. Rather, it should allow for multiple improvisations on a theme. After we have crafted a vision we can all support, we need to determine how to communicate it to the world beyond our small professional circle. We need to develop a message that is credible and clear. This will be essential when we get to step 4. First, however, we must think about increasing our leadership potential.

Step 2: Developing Leaders

It will take a strong cadre of leaders to get it right for children's library services in the future. We will need capable, charismatic, committed children's librarians who can implement change in their own communities and people who can take the struggle to larger arenas.

In his book *The Tipping Point: How Little Things Can Make a Big Difference* (2000), Malcolm Gladwell speculates about the causes of sudden, unexpected social change—fashion trends, innovations in children's television, sudden upswings or downturns in crime. He pinpoints three rules that explain these social epidemics: the law of the few, "stickiness," and context. I will talk about stickiness and context later. The law of the few has relevance for our thinking about leadership.

Gladwell found that there were a few critical people behind all of the mass social phenomena he investigated. Eventually, large numbers of people participated in these events or trends, but at the beginning there were just a few. Gladwell places these few people into three categories: connectors, mavens, and salespeople. We need all three to create the right libraries for future kids.

Connectors are the virtuosos of the Rolodex, the people who know everybody. They are the supreme networkers who find making social connections both easy and natural. They often occupy places in overlapping worlds. In this group I think of people like library advocate Virginia Matthews, who seems equally at home at library conferences and in legislative offices; or Bill Morris, longtime head of marketing for children's books at HarperCollins, who knows everybody in the Association for Library Service to Children (ALSC), the International Reading Association, the National Council of Teachers of English, and children's book publishing; or Susan Roman, former executive director of ALSC, whose fund-raising and networking activities on behalf of the association have forged contacts within the leadership ranks of Head Start, corporate foundations, children's museums, and public broadcasting; or Penny Markey, youth services coordinator at Los Angeles County Public Library, who knows everybody in the county who is involved in children's advocacy.

We will need those connectors to start a revolution in library services for children. We will also need the people Gladwell calls mavens. Mavens collect information. They are often experts on a particular topic. They are also passionate about their area of expertise and share their knowledge eagerly. Think about the friend you automatically go to for a restaurant recommendation or advice on a new car purchase. You know that his or her information will be reliable.

We need to identify mavens with particular information specialties who can keep us abreast of critical issues. Is there a library school professor who can apprise us of research that links libraries with children's reading abilities? Who is the best source for current data on children's demographics, library usage, or library budgets? Who knows how to track legislation related to children and libraries? Who is most likely to be aware of innovative good practices in children's library programs around the country?

In some cases, we can depend on institutional offices such as the ALA Office of Research or the ALA Washington office to act as information mavens for all of us. However, we will probably need to annoint many informal mavens and empower them to keep us supplied with the data we need to start our revolution in children's library service.

The connector and maven roles come naturally to many children's librarians. The salesperson role is a little less comfortable for many of us. Salespeople are the great communicators. They are the ones who will take our vision out into the world and persuade people to believe in it. The best salespeople are natural optimists who genuinely believe in their product or message. They tend to be charismatic leaders whose personalities compel us to follow them—or at least to trust them.

Although children's librarians believe in the goodness of their work, they are often too defensive about it to be good salespeople. They are able to motivate a child to read a great book but feel less sure about their ability to motivate another adult to support good library service for kids. They are often powerful storytellers but feel more reticent when their story deals with issues of policy and administration instead of tricksters and giants. We can learn to do this, though. We have the basic communication skills; we just need to apply them to a different audience with a different purpose.

We can begin to think of ourselves as connectors, mavens, and salespeople—all different kinds of leaders. Then we need to try these roles on and encourage our colleagues to do the same. If each of us found one role that fit well and practiced it, we would have the cadre we need to begin creating those future libraries for future kids.

The next step will involve extending the discussion and winning allies.

Step 3: Winning Allies

Talking to ourselves is something else children's librarians are very good at. We genuinely like each other, and we like getting together to talk about our work. However, it is clear that we will need to extend the discussion beyond our inner circle if we really want to get it right for future kids. We need to win allies who will come to care as much about good libraries for children as we do.

We can identify some obvious categories of people we want on our side.

library administrators

leaders in the Public Library Association and ALA Council

influential staff and members of the Urban Libraries Council

library advocates in organizations like Libraries for the Future

foundation staff

elected and appointed officials at all levels of government

key people in education

media spokespeople

gatekeepers and key informants in the communities where
    we work

children's advocacy organizations like the Children's Defense
    Fund and the Children's Partnership

philanthropists

public interest lawyers

marketing experts

kids

Each group will require a different strategy, but we must find ways to talk to them about the importance of libraries for the child reader, the child of the Information Age, or the child in the community. We have to tell our story so that they will want to listen. Then we must be ready with ways for all of these people to take action. We might have to create organizations for them to join, like the library Friends groups we have now. Or we might find it more effective to develop loose networks and project-oriented task forces. What is essential is that we win allies and give them jobs to do. Maybe some of our new supporters can help us with step 4.

Step 4: Spreading the Word

It's a cliche in library circles: "The library is the best-kept secret in town." This has got to change if we want to make big changes in library services for kids. We need to get much better at spreading the word. People need to know what a good job we are doing now and what a fabulous job we will do in the future, with their help and support.

Some of this can be accomplished through more effective public relations efforts. In our heart of hearts, we know that our photocopied brochures and the public service announcements that air at midnight are not doing the job. When we talk about doing it better, we usually blame the lack of money for our failure to do more creative and effective promotion. True, more money would enable us to contract with more established consultants, hire better production companies, design better graphics, and buy more useful air time. We should make every effort to raise the kind of money that would make really excellent promotion possible both for local library services and for national public awareness campaigns.

Money isn't the only answer, however. In *The Tipping Point*, Gladwell talks about the importance of "stickiness." For an idea or a service or a product to catch on, it needs to be so memorable that it sticks in the mind and so irresistible that it stirs people to action. This can be an advertising slogan: "Got milk?" "Winston tastes good like a cigarette should." "You deserve a break today." Stickiness can be built into a concept, such as the *Sesame Street* notion that television could teach little kids to read. Gladwell describes the endless research and tinkering *Sesame Street*'s producers have engaged in to keep the show sticky, to keep preschoolers watching and learning.

The secret to getting the right stickiness is often a matter of a tiny adjustment in language, operations, or appearance. *Sesame Street* creators found that all they needed to keep kids' attention on live actors was to add one interesting fantasy character—Big Bird. Many commentators have observed that the secret of the stickiness of the old Winston slogan was the ungrammatical substitution of "like" for "as." As Gladwell says, "There is a simple way to package information that, under the right circumstances, can make it irresistible. All you have to do is find it" (Gladwell 2000, 132).

So we need to look for the sticky messages—the sound bites and slogans, the images and metaphors—that will communicate our vision of future libraries for future kids. ALA's Public Information Office has found, for example, that an effective way to communicate our belief that it is better to give children information literacy skills than to install the imperfect software filters that exist today is to say: "We think kids can be trained to be their own filters." We need to develop more messages like that and put them in the hands of the great salespeople among us and our supporters.

If we are effective in spreading the good news about what we do for kids in libraries, and if we are convincing about our plans for the future, we will find that step 5—changing the policies that affect library service for children—is much easier to accomplish.

Step 5: Changing Policy

Public policy is a general term that refers to government decisions and actions that deal with matters of public concern (Cochran and Malone 1999, 1). Public policy emerges through a complex process of influence, negotiation, decision making, and bureaucratic implementation. Public policy is created at all levels of government. Much of it affects library service for children both directly and indirectly.

At the national level, as I write this book, there is no policy that provides funding directly for public library service for children. Children's librarians can compete for the money that is passed through state library agencies for Library Services and Technology Act (LSTA) funding and for the various programs available through the Institute of Museum and Library Services (IMLS). There is no program or legislation, however, that earmarks money for public library service for children. This is a policy gap we might want to address.

The legislative issue that affects the library most directly at the moment is Internet access for children, but we should be alert to other items on the national policy agenda as well. If a law affects children, it will affect children's librarians sooner or later.

Librarians should be monitoring legislation that deals with early childhood development and education. As I noted earlier in this book, public libraries are the natural agencies to take the lead on emergent literacy initiatives. We need to be written into the bills, or the money will go to organizations that are far less competent than we are to guide parents and caregivers in appropriate literacy development practices for young children.

At the state level, policies regarding school curriculum affect children and the libraries that serve them, both school and public. Some states are also experimenting with Internet filtering legislation. In California, librarians are working very hard to get libraries included in various legislative packages supporting youth development.

Policy developed at the local level tends to have the most direct effect on library services for children because almost all of us get the biggest chunk of funding from local government. Budget allocations are the most obvious place where the interests of children are served or ignored, and many children's librarians have become effective advocates in this arena. However, there are other local policies that affect children's access to library services. The "unattended child" policies in effect in some public libraries prevent children from using the library unless an adult accompanies them. More Internet filtering policies are imposed by local library boards than by federal mandate.

How can children's librarians and their network of supporters for better future libraries for future kids ensure that policy at all levels of government supports what we are trying to do? It is easiest to imagine this at the local level, where the results of lobbying are more obvious and immediate, than at state and national levels. However, we do have policy experts in the ALA Washington office and elsewhere who will work on our behalf.

I talked earlier about Malcolm Gladwell's notion of the tipping point and the factors that contribute to sudden, sweeping social change. I mentioned "the law of the few" that tries to account for the kind of people who instigate new trends and social movements. I discussed the stickiness factor in connection with marketing. Gladwell's third rule is context; it's all about timing and critical mass. There are moments when all the conditions are right for change; we need to recognize those situations and be ready to act.

Anthony Downs (1972) is a political scientist who formulated a classic theory called the issue-attention cycle. The idea is that key domestic problems move in and out of the public eye all the time. The longer an issue stays at the forefront of public attention, the more likely it is to command political action. Downs describes five typical stages in this cycle. At the pre-problem stage, a major problem has developed, but the only people who are aware of it are a few policy experts or special interest groups. The second stage is "alarmed discovery and euphoric enthusiasm." Usually some dramatic event attracts media attention at this point, and politicians react with expressions of alarm. The special interest groups involved with the issue are euphoric at this point because they think the politicians might act at last. At the third stage, politicians realize how much it would cost to actually solve the problem, and they begin to back off from the kinds of action they may have promised during the second stage. The fourth stage is a gradual decline of public interest. People may be less enthusiastic about solutions when they understand their cost. They may be more interested in new issues that command the head-lines. Only the hard-core advocates are still engaged with the issue. Finally, in the post-problem stage, the issue has moved off the center stage. Some programs and policies may have been put into place; and the insiders, bureaucrats, and special interest groups will have a platform for action.

The lesson for us is that we need to be ready at stage 2, when there is intense public interest in an issue we care about. When the newscasters report on children's failure to read, we need to be ready with library programs that support early childhood literacy. When politicians point with alarm to youth violence and alienation, we need to demonstrate how public libraries can support positive youth development with sound after-school programs. When conservative talk radio hosts create hysteria about children and the Internet, we need to be ready to persuade people that public libraries can guide children and families safely through cyberspace.

Once we learn to speak with authority and conviction about policies that work for children, we can take our places at the table where decisions are made and speak truth to power.

Step 6: Changing Organizations

The thought of changing the organizations we work for can seem even more daunting than changing national policies. This is not surprising. Every public library I know is structured as a bureaucracy; and bureaucracies were designed for permanence, not for change. The folks who work in the lower or middle ranks aren't the only ones who despair of making significant changes in their organization. Ask any library director how easy it is to move an organization in new directions or to change an entrenched organizational culture.

And yet public libraries must change if we are going to achieve the vision of excellent library services for children. Children's departments or chil-dren's rooms are embedded in a bigger organization. There are some things that we can do for children on our own, but for more systemic changes, the library must change as well. Here is a short list of changes that need to be made in our public libraries if we are going to accomplish even a small part of our vision:

new career ladders for children's librarians

new position descriptions for specialists in different aspects
of library services for children: early childhood specialists,

computer technicians, homework center aides, community
outreach workers, and many more

new reward structures that will entice the best and the brightest
to become children's librarians

family-friendly operating hours

family-friendly and child-friendly facilities

child-friendly library catalogs

better channels of communication between children's library
staff and administrative staff

Some communities might decide to split off their children's library services from the general public library services in order to focus on children's needs. I know of at least two branch libraries that function as libraries for children and youth, and they seem to work very well in their communities.

Organizational change is difficult, but it does happen. Imagine what an innovation it was to designate space, staff, and resources for those first children's rooms in American libraries over one hundred years ago. Now let's consider how we might accomplish the kinds of organizational change we would like to see in our public libraries on behalf of future kids.

First of all, if we have taken steps 1 and 2 seriously, we will be ready with a vision, a plan, and the leaders to articulate and implement them. Some of us may have moved out of leadership roles in the children's library community into more general positions of leadership as library directors, deans, and ALA presidents. We did it before, and we can do it again. We will have recruited allies to our cause and put policies in place to support the organizational changes we require.

It is also possible to effect organizational change from the middle or even the bottom of the hierarchy. All organizations generate informal leaders as well as formal leaders who occupy supervisory and administrative roles. The informal leaders are instrumental in generating the organizational culture. All of us can work to create a culture that is welcoming to children and families, that supports the work we do, that nurtures our creativity and commitment. To do this effectively, we must do our own work well and support our colleagues in their efforts. We need to be effective salespeople for our vision and communicate its importance through our behavior as well as our words.

We must also enlist the cooperation of an important institution—the library school—and work to implement changes in that arena.

Step 7: Changing Library Education

Actually, they don't call it library school in very many places any more. At UCLA, where I work, it's the Department of Information Studies, located in the Graduate School of Education and Information Studies. Never mind. We still have ALA accreditation, and we still educate librarians—in addition to archivists, information scientists, and information professionals whose job titles are still evolving.

These graduate programs need to evolve to support changes in library services for children. First, they need to recruit far more children's librarians than they do at present. Second, they need to ensure that their curriculum provides the basic knowledge that new children's librarians will need to bring to their first jobs. Finally, they need to become more aggressive about offering continuing education to help children's librarians upgrade their skills and knowledge.

Library schools cannot accomplish the recruiting objective by themselves. The profession as a whole needs to share the responsibility for this. Our national associations must mount an aggressive recruitment campaign that targets the areas of most critical need, children's librarians being the first of these. We need to generate bountiful scholarship funds, through public policy initiatives and private philanthropy. Then public libraries must offer salaries and working conditions that are competitive in a hot job market.

Professionals working for government will probably never earn the salaries that attract entrepreneurs to Silicon Valley, but we can offer much more than we do at present. We can also ensure that our children's librarians enjoy intangible rewards such as job satisfaction, opportunities for promotion, opportunities to serve, opportunities to grow and develop, the respect of our peers and our community, the ability to make decisions about the aspects of our job that affect us most, and good working conditions.

Those of us who are children's librarians should think about the image we project to those who would come after us. Do we appear happy with our profession and our jobs? Do we tell children how much we like our work, thereby planting a seed that may flower into a future children's librarian? Do we recruit promising clerical and paraprofessional staff in our libraries?

Most of the good library schools in this country reevaluate their curriculum constantly and try to offer courses that are relevant to the jobs their students will take upon graduation. They are generally forward thinking and responsive to the needs of the marketplace. There are some significant barriers, however, when it comes to meeting the needs of future children's librarians.

The first of these is a shortfall in tenured professors who specialize in children's services. Not every library school in the country has even one tenured professor who focuses on children's library services. Only a handful have more than one.

The consequence is that too many library schools must rely on temporary adjunct faculty to teach the courses devoted to children's library work. Most of them are dedicated, competent professionals who bring current work experiences into the classroom, but as adjunct faculty they are marginal in the overall governance of the program. They have little input into curriculum design. They are usually not available to serve as advisors to students. They tend to have more limited office hours and fewer informal contacts with students outside of class.

A highly visible tenured professor—or, better yet, a critical mass of tenured professors—is more likely to be able to provide leadership and support for library school students who want to specialize in children's services. They may even recruit students who thought they wanted to be catalogers or archivists or university librarians to the noble profession of children's librarian. Tenured faculty also introduce new courses. If we want courses for future children's librarians in multicultural children's literature, services for babies and toddlers, marketing to children, or outreach to diverse populations—we will need tenured faculty to design and teach them.

So more of us will need to get that Ph.D. and embark on careers as academicians. The future of library education may depend on it.

Step 8: Doing Research

I frequently get calls from colleagues who want to know if there is any research that supports the value of summer reading programs, youth participation, intergenerational programming, or other library services for young people. They are usually working on a grant proposal or a budget request and need justification for their project. Unfortunately, there is very little research that backs up what they want to do.

The reasons for the lack of research related to library services for children are both very obvious and very subtle. The obvious reason is that, as I pointed out in step 7 above, there are too few tenured professors specializing in children's services. Professors are expected to do research as well as to teach classes and to participate in the governance of their academic unit. In more research-oriented universities, they really do "publish or perish." Doing research and having it published in prestigious, scholarly journals is key to getting tenure and being promoted. You would expect, therefore, that at least the handful of us who specialize in children's library services would publish research that our colleagues in public libraries would find useful.

The more subtle reason for the scarcity of research about children and libraries is the perception in some academic circles that this is a less valid topic for scholarly inquiry than others. This perception dampens the spirits of untenured assistant professors looking to publish research that will establish their reputation and build the foundation for their tenure cases.

For many of us, tenure and promotion depend on articles published in refereed journals. These are scholarly journals that use peer review as the basis for accepting articles. An article is sent to as many as five reviewers who evaluate it on the basis of its methodology and findings, originality, and contributions to existing knowledge. It is certainly possible to publish articles about research related to children in the general interest peer-reviewed journals such as *Library Quarterly* and *Library and Information Science Research*. Unfortunately, few practitioners ever see those journals, and the research findings are lost to those who could really use them. Articles published in *School Library Journal*, on the other hand, are read by children's librarians but may actually detract from an assistant professor's tenure case.

Some of us in academia do, in fact, publish research that you can use (if you can find it). Carol Kuhlthau's research on the information-seeking behavior of students has helped many librarians rethink how they guide young people with homework assignments. Mary Kay Chelton and Melissa Gross have done groundbreaking research on the ways in which librarians interact with young people at the reference desk. Eliza Dresang is reconceptualizing children's literature in ways that have enormous consequence for collection development and readers' advisory work. My own research has resulted in tools that children's and young adult librarians can use to evaluate their work and in a new understanding of children's information needs. Christine Jenkins's and Anne Lundin's historical research is reclaiming our past and helping us understand our origins and traditions.

Some children's library practitioners have collaborated with academicians on research projects. Leslie Holt left academia to become the youth services coordinator at St. Louis Public Library. She has participated in research being conducted at her library on the economic benefits of library services. As the program officer for the DeWitt Wallace-Reader's Digest

Fund's libraries and youth development project, Elaine Meyers has generated some useful information about how we might market our library services better to young people. Penny Markey and I worked together on a study of parent perceptions of the Los Angeles County Public Library's summer reading program that we published in *The Journal of Youth Services* (Walter and Markey 1997). Some children's librarians contract with experts to do research-based evaluations of grant-funded projects; more of those studies need to be published and made available to others.

I see the greatest research needs in two areas. One is the codification of best practices in our field. We need more than anecdotal evidence and common sense to determine what works and what doesn't. The second need is for tangible evidence of the outcomes of our work. This would include rigorous studies to establish the results of our basic services: summer reading programs, reference and readers' advisory services, Internet access and instruction, preschool story programs. Ideally, the research would incorporate both quantitative and qualitative methods and have a national scope. Some longitudinal studies would also be required. This kind of research is expensive, but if it is done well, it will arm children's librarians around the country with evidence that service to children is important and has results.

All children's librarians need to have enough research skill to accomplish step 9, evaluating our work.

Step 9: Evaluating Our Work

Systematic evaluation of our work will improve library services for children. We need to document our productivity in order to be accountable for the resources given to us to do the job. We need to know if we are meeting our own objectives. As reflective professionals, children's librarians need to be constantly monitoring their own performance and the needs of their clients. Do our services still match the children's needs? Can we improve our operations or practices? Can we do things more effectively? Should we still be offering the same services? We can't answer those questions without having some data about the work we do.

As competent managers, most children's librarians do try to evaluate their services. Yet there is a subtle strain of resistance to formal evaluation that runs through our profession. Many of us believe that the most important services we provide are intangible and therefore unquantifiable. How do you measure a child's delight at story time, the satisfaction of reading the right book at the right time, or the sense of mastery a child feels when she has learned to search the Internet successfully? Others say they are overworked and have no time for ambitious evaluation efforts.

Output Measures for Public Library Service to Children (Walter 1992) gives children's librarians some easy-to-use tools for defining and measuring the outputs—the tangible results—of their work, along with tips for interpreting and communicating the results. It includes measurement techniques that any librarian could adopt to evaluate aspects of services to children.

Other approaches to evaluation come from management strategies such as total quality management (TQM). TQM was developed in the 1930s by an American industrial engineer, W. Edwards Deming. It stresses continuous improvement of an organization's processes. One technique TQM advocates often use is the quality circle, in which workers assigned to the same task meet regularly to identify and solve problems. Another technique used in most TQM systems is benchmarking, taking quantitative measures of productivity and quality at regular intervals (Sashkin and Kiser 1993; Schmidt and Finnigan 1992; Shaughnessy 1993). Where TQM has been most effective, its practices have been seamlessly integrated into the regular operations of the organization. This appears to be a common element in successful evaluation strategies; they need to become second nature, business as usual, rather than special activities that are laid on top of regular duties.

Children's librarians do good work. Evaluation allows us to prove it. It is important to remember, as we calculate the annual children's fill rate or design a parent satisfaction survey, that children will be the ultimate winners if we play the evaluation game. This is the final step in getting it right for children's library services.

Step 10: Keeping the Focus

I have encouraged children's librarians to be networkers, information mavens, salespeople, politicians, diplomats, researchers, teachers, managers, and statisticians as we work to achieve the dream of excellent future libraries for future kids. Now I am going to insist that we stay focused on children all the time. We are not working so hard just to make the library directors and politicians happy, although that may be a consequence of our work. We are not learning new skills and gaining new knowledge just to enhance our own professional development, although that will inevitably result. We do what we do to benefit the children.

We must keep our eyes on the prize. The goal is good libraries for the children of today and better libraries for the children of tomorrow. We must constantly remember what excellent library services can do for children. We give children hope, dreams, words to think with, inspiration, information, positive role models, cultural validation, self-esteem, personal attention, a listening ear, opportunities to participate in the life of their community, moments of delight, answers to questions, and questions to answer. What other public agency can offer so much?

Afterword
Five Laws of Children's Librarianship

IN THE INTRODUCTION TO THIS BOOK, I acknowledged my intellectual debt to Walt Crawford and Michael Gorman, whose book *Future Libraries: Dreams, Madness, and Reality* (1995) started me thinking about future libraries for future kids. When I finished writing the last chapter, I knew that my work was still not complete. In a sense, it never will be, not until we can say "all the children are well."

That time will come, I believe. But even after the vision has been achieved, children's librarians will still need to do the work they do best and continue to meet the challenges of an ever-changing world. To help those future children's librarians think about their vocation, I have formulated five laws of children's librarianship, based on the original five laws of librarianship developed by Ranganathan in 1931. Here they are:

Libraries serve the reading interests and information needs of all children, directly and through service to parents and other adults who are involved with the lives of children.

Children's librarians provide the right book or information for the right child at the right time in the right place.

Children's librarians are advocates for children's access to books, information, information technology, and ideas.

Children's librarians promote children's literacy in all media.

Children's librarians honor their traditions and create the future.

Appendix

Competencies for Librarians Serving Children in Public Libraries

Adopted by the Board of the Association
for Library Service to Children in 1999

I. Knowledge of Client Group

1. Understands theories of infant, child, and adolescent learning and development and their implications for library service.
2. Recognizes the effects of societal developments on the needs of children.
3. Assesses the community regularly and systematically to identify community needs, tastes, and resources.
4. Identifies clients with special needs as a basis for designing and implementing services, following American Disabilities Act (ADA) and state and local regulations where appropriate.
5. Recognizes the needs of an ethnically diverse community.
6. Understands and responds to the needs of parents, caregivers, and other adults who use the resources of the children's department.
7. Creates an environment in the children's area which provides for enjoyable and convenient use of library resources.
8. Maintains regular communication with other agencies, institutions, and organizations serving children in the community.

II. Administrative and Management Skills

1. Participates in all aspects of the library's planning process to represent and support children's services.
2. Sets long- and short-range goals, objectives, and priorities.
3. Analyzes the costs of library services to children in order to develop, justify, administer/manage, and evaluate a budget.
4. Writes job descriptions and interviews, trains, encourages continuing education, and evaluates staff who work with children, con-

sulting with other library administrations as indicated in library personnel policy.

5. Demonstrates problem-solving, decision-making, and mediation techniques.
6. Delegates responsibility appropriately and supervises staff constructively.
7. Documents and evaluates services.
8. Identifies outside sources of funding and writes effective grant applications.

III. Communication Skills

1. Defines and communicates the needs of children so that administrators, other library staff, and members of the larger community understand the basis for children's services.
2. Demonstrates interpersonal skills in meeting with children, parents, staff, and community.
3. Adjusts to the varying demands of writing planning documents, procedures, guidelines, press releases, memoranda, reports, grant applications, annotations, and reviews in all formats, including print and electronic.
4. Speaks effectively when addressing individuals, as well as small and large groups.
5. Applies active listening skills.
6. Conducts productive formal and informal reference interviews.
7. Communicates constructively with "problem patrons."

IV. Materials and Collection Development

A. Knowledge of Materials

1. Demonstrates a knowledge and appreciation of children's literature, periodicals, audiovisual materials, Web sites and other electronic media, and other materials that constitute a diverse, current, and relevant children's collection.
2. Keeps abreast of new materials and those for retrospective purchase by consulting a wide variety of reviewing sources and publishers' catalog, including those of small presses; by attending professional meetings; and by reading, viewing, and listening.

3. Is aware of adult reference materials and other library resources that may serve the needs of children and their caregivers.

B. Ability to Select Appropriate Materials and Develop a Children's Collection.

1. Evaluates and recommends collection development, selection and weeding policies for children's materials consistent with the mission and policies of the parent library and the ALA Library Bill of Rights, and applies these policies in acquiring and weeding materials for or management of the children's collection.
2. Acquires materials that reflect the ethnic diversity of the community, as well as the need of children to become familiar with other ethnic groups and cultures.
3. Understands and applies criteria for evaluating the content and artistic merit of children's materials in all genres and formats.
4. Keeps abreast of current issues in children's materials collections and formulates a professional philosophy with regard to these issues.
5. Demonstrates a knowledge of technical services, cataloging and indexing procedures, and practices relating to children's materials.

C. Ability to Provide Customers with Appropriate Materials and Information

1. Connects children to the wealth of library resources, enabling them to use libraries effectively.
2. Matches children and their families with materials appropriate to their interests and abilities.
3. Provides help where needed, respects children's right to browse, and answers questions regardless of their nature or purpose.
4. Assists and instructs children in information gathering and research as appropriate.
5. Understands and applies search strategies to give children full and equitable access to information from the widest possible range of sources, such as children's and adult reference works, indexes, catalogs, electronic resources, information and referral files, and interlibrary loan networks.

6. Compiles and maintains information about community resources so that children and adults working with children can be referred to appropriate sources of assistance.
7. Works with library technical services to guarantee that the children's collection is organized and accessed for the easiest possible use.
8. Creates bibliographies, book talks, displays, electronic documents, and other special tools to increase access to library resources and motivate their use.

V. Programming Skills

1. Designs, promotes, executes, and evaluates programs for children of all ages, based on their developmental needs and interests and the goals of the library.
2. Presents a variety of programs or brings in skilled resource people to present these programs, including storytelling, book talks, book discussions, puppet programs, and other appropriate activities.
3. Provides outreach programs commensurate with community needs and library goals and objectives.
4. Establishes programs and services for parents, individuals and agencies providing child care, and other professionals in the community who work with children.

VI. Advocacy, Public Relations, and Networking Skills

1. Promotes an awareness of and support for meeting children's library and information needs through all media.
2. Considers the opinions and requests of children in the development and evaluation of library services.
3. Ensures that children have full access to library materials, resources, and services as prescribed by the Library Bill of Rights.
4. Acts as liaison with other agencies in the community serving children, including other libraries and library system.
5. Develops cooperative programs between the public library, schools, and other community agencies.
6. Extends library services to children and groups of children presently unserved.

7. Uses effective public relations techniques and media to publicize library activities.
8. Develops policies and procedures applying to children's services based on federal, state, and local law where appropriate.
9. Understands library governance and the political process and lobbies on behalf of children's services.

VII. Professionalism and Professional Development

1. Acknowledges the legacy of children's librarianship, its place in the context of librarianship as a whole, and past contributions to the profession.
2. Keeps abreast of current trends and emerging technologies, issues, and research in librarianship, child development, education, and allied fields.
3. Practices self-evaluation.
4. Conveys a nonjudgmental attitude toward patrons and their requests.
5. Demonstrates an understanding of and respect for diversity in cultural and ethnic values.
6. Knows and practices the American Library Association's Code of Ethics.
7. Preserves confidentiality in interchanges with patrons.
8. Works with library educators to meet needs of library school students and promote professional association scholarships.
9. Participates in professional organizations to strengthen skills, interact with fellow professionals, and contribute to the profession.
10. Understands that professional development and continuing education are activities to be pursued throughout one's career.

SOURCE: Association for Library Service to Children. 1999.
<www.ala.org/alsc/competencies.html>

References

Adler, Patricia A., and Peter Adler. 1998. *Peer power: Preadolescent culture and identity.* New Brunswick, N.J.: Rutgers University Press.

Alter, Jonathan. 1998. It's 4:00 p.m.: Do you know where your children are? *Newsweek*, 27 April, 33.

American Association of School Librarians and Association for Educational Communications and Technology. 1998. *Information power: Building partnerships for learning.* Chicago: American Library Association.

American Association of University Women Educational Foundation. 1998. *Gender gaps: Where schools still fail our children.* Washington, D.C.: American Association of University Women.

American Library Association. 1999. 700+ great sites: Amazing, spectacular, mysterious, wonderful web sites for kids and the adults who care about them. <www.ala.org/parentspage/greatsites/amazing.html> Last accessed 5 August 1999.

____. Office for Intellectual Freedom. 1999. Most frequently challenged books of 1998. <www.ala.org/bbooks/challeng.html/#mfcb> Last accessed 18 August 1999.

Anderson, Nick. 1998. Miami: Bilingual classes for all. *Los Angeles Times*, 25 May, A1 and A24.

Annenberg Public Policy Center, University of Pennsylvania. 1999. The Internet and the family. <www.appcpenn.org/internet/> Last accessed 12 July 1999.

Annie E. Casey Foundation. 1999. Kids count data online. <www.aecf.org> Last accessed 31 July 1999.

Annual conference placement center stats. 1999. *American Libraries* 30 (7): 84.

Aries, Philipe. 1962. *Centuries of childhood.* New York: Random House.

Avner, Jane A. 1997. Home schoolers: A forgotten clientele? In *School Library Journal's best: A reader for children's, young adult, and school librarians,* edited by Lillian N. Gerhardt. New York: Neal-Schuman. Originally published in *School Library Journal* 35 (July 1989).

Bader, Barbara. 1997. Only the best: The hits and misses of Anne Carroll Moore. *Horn Book* 73 (5): 520-28.

Baker, Augusta, and Ellin Greene. 1987. *Storytelling art and technique.* 2d ed. New York: Bowker.

Barstow, Barbara, and Penny Markey. 1997. Mix it up: 6 ways to rethink tired summer reading programs. *School Library Journal* 43 (11): 30-33.

Becht, Debbie, Kevin Taglang, and Anthony Wilhelm. 1999. The digital divide and the U.S. Hispanic population. *The Digital Beat* 1 (13). <www.benton.org/DigitalBeat/db080699.html> Last accessed 31 August 1999.

Bellah, Robert N. et al. 1985. *Habits of the heart: Individualism and commitment in American life.* Berkeley, Calif.: University of California Press.

Bennetts, Leslie. 1999. The digital divide. *Family PC,* August, 90-95.

Benton Foundation. *Buildings, books, and bytes: Libraries and communities in the digital age.* 1996. Washington, D.C.: Benton Foundation.

Berger, Peter L., and Richard John Neuhaus. 1977. *To empower people: The role of mediating structures in public policy.* Washington, D.C.: American Enterprise Institute.

Bertot, John Carlo, and Charles R. McClure. 1998. The 1998 national survey of U.S. public library outlet Internet connectivity: Summary results. Chicago: American Library Association/Office for Information Technology Policy. <www.ala.org/oitp/survey98.html> Last accessed 14 July 1999.

Bierlein, Louann. 1997. The charter school movement. In *New schools for a new century: The redesign of urban education*, edited by Diane Ravitch and Joseph P. Viteritti. New Haven, Conn.: Yale University Press.

Blatchford, Mary Lee, Marjorie Ann Crammer, Susan Paznekas, and Stacey Aldrich. 1998. Quality of reference service to children: A pilot study from Maryland. Reported at Public Library Association Conference, Kansas City, Mo.

Blume, Judy. 1974. *Blubber.* New York: Simon & Schuster Books for Young Readers.

Boone, Jill. 2000. Helping homeschoolers: What libraries can do. *California Libraries* 10 (4): 2.

Borgman, Christine L. et al. 1995. Children's searching behavior on browsing and keyword online catalogs: The science library catalog project. *Journal of the American Society for Information Science* 46 (9): 663-84.

Boyer, Ernest L. 1991. *Ready to learn: A mandate for the nation.* Princeton, N.J.: Carnegie Foundation for the Advancement of Teaching/ Princeton University Press.

Bradsher, Keith. 1999. Murder trial of 13-year-old puts focus on Michigan law. *New York Times*, 31 October, A21.

Bransford, John D., Ann L. Brown, and Rodney R. Cocking, eds. 1999. *How people learn: Brain, mind, experience, and school.* Washington, D.C.: National Academy Press.

Braun, Stephen. 1999. Real mayhem renews cry against video game kind. *Los Angeles Times*, 1 May, A1 and A14.

Bredekamp, Sue, ed. 1987. *Developmentally appropriate practice in early childhood programs serving children from birth through age 8.* Expanded edition. Washington, D.C.: National Association for the Education of Young Children.

Brooks, Bruce. 1992. *What hearts?* New York: HarperCollins.

Brown, Malore Ingrid. 1996. *Multicultural youth materials selection.* Ph.D. diss., University of Wisconsin, Milwaukee. Abstract in *Dissertation Abstracts International* 57:4970A.

Byars, Betsy. 1988. *The burning questions of Bingo Brown.* New York: Viking.

Cart, Julie. 1999. Residents struggle for closure after Columbine carnage. *Los Angeles Times*, 7 August, A8.

Cassell, Justine, and Henry Jenkins. 1998. Chess for girls? Feminism and computer games. In *From Barbie to Mortal Kombat: Gender and computer games*, edited by Justine Cassell and Henry Jenkins. Cambridge, Mass.: MIT Press.

Censorship watch. 1999. *American Libraries* 30 (6): 31.

Chaiet, Donna. 1998. *The safe zone: A kid's guide to personal safety.* New York: Beech Tree.

Children Now. 1998. Child care in the United States. Fact sheet. <www.childrennow.org/economics/childcareus.html> Last accessed 4 August 1999.

Children's Defense Fund. 1999a. *Child care basics.* Washington, D.C.: Children's Defense Fund.

_____. 1999b. *Key facts: Essential information on child care, early education, and school-age care.* Washington, D.C.: Children's Defense Fund.

_____. 2000. *School-age care basics.* Washington, D.C.: Children's Defense Fund.

The Children's Partnership. 1999. Kids and families online. <www.childrens partnership.org/bbar/kids.html> Last accessed 12 July 1999.

Chmielewski, Dawn C. 1999. Public access. *Orange County Register*, 27 July, 9.

Chu, Clara M. 1999. Immigrant children mediators (ICM): Bridging the literacy gap in immigrant communities. Conference proceedings. 65th IFLA Council and General Conference, Bangkok, Thailand. <www.ifla.org/IV/ifla65/65cp.htm> Last accessed 4 August 1999.

Clark, Marilyn L. 1997. The public library and homework help. *Public Libraries* 36 (1): 19-20.

Clemetson, Lynette. 1998. Caught in the cross-fire. *Newsweek*, 13 December, 38-39.

Cochran, Charles L., and Eloise R. Malone. 1999. *Public policy: Perspectives and choices.* 2d ed. Boston: McGraw-Hill.

Colburn, Nell. 1994. 10 tips for an outstanding children's collection. *School Library Journal* 40 (9): 130-33.

Coley, Richard J., John Cradler, and Penelope K. Engel. 1997. Computers and classrooms: The status of technology in U.S. schools. ETS Policy Information Report. Princeton, N.J.: ETS Policy Information Center. <www.ets.org/research/pic/compclass.html> Last accessed 3 September 1999.

Conly, Jane. 1993. *Crazy lady!* New York: HarperCollins.

Connor, Jane Gardner. 1990. *Children's library services handbook.* Phoenix, Ariz.: Oryx.

Coretta Scott King award. 1999. American Library Association. <www.ala. org/srrt/csking/index.html> Last accessed 20 July 1999.

Cormier, Robert. 1993. *The chocolate war.* New York: Knopf.

Council on Interracial Books for Children. 1980. *Guidelines for selecting bias-free textbooks and storybooks.* New York: Council on Interracial Books for Children.

Crawford, Walt, and Michael Gorman. 1995. *Future libraries: Dreams, madness, and reality.* Chicago: American Library Association.

Cross, Gary. 1997. *Kids' stuff: Toys and the changing world of American childhood.* Cambridge, Mass.: Harvard University Press.

Cummins, Julie. 1999. More than meets the eye. *School Library Journal* 45 (7): 27-29.

Curran, Charles. 1990. Information literacy and the public librarian. *Public Libraries* 29 (6): 349-53.

Dalaker, Joseph, and Mary Naifeh. 1998. *U.S. Bureau of the Census, Current Population Reports, Series P60-201, Poverty in the United States: 1997.* Washington, D.C.: Government Printing Office.

De Becker, Gavin. 1999. *Protecting the gift: Keeping children and teenagers safe and parents sane.* New York: Bantam.

Del Vecchio, Gene. 1997. *Creating ever-cool: A marketer's guide to a kid's heart.* Greatna, La.: Pelican.

Demi. 1998. *The Dalai Lama: A biography of the Tibetan spiritual and political leader.* New York: Holt.

Demos, John. 1986. *Past, present, and personal: The family and the life course in American history.* New York: Oxford University Press.

DeWitt Wallace-Reader's Digest Fund. *Public libraries as partners in youth development.* 1999. New York: DeWitt Wallace-Reader's Digest Fund.

Donahue, Patricia L. et al. 1999. *NAEP 1998 reading report card for the nation and the states.* Washington, D.C.: National Center for Education Statistics. <nces.ed.gov/nationsreportcard/pubs/main1998/1999500. shtml> Last accessed 26 July 1999.

Dowd, Frances Smardo. 1991. *Latchkey children in the library and community.* Phoenix, Ariz.: Oryx.

Downs, Anthony. 1972. The issue-attention cycle. *The Public Interest.* 28: 38-50.

Doyle, Christina S. *Information literacy in an information society: A concept for the information age.* Syracuse, New York: ERIC Clearing House on Information and Technology, Syracuse University.

Dr. Laura crusades against ALA. 1999. *American Libraries* 30 (6): 9-10.

Dresang, Eliza T. 1997. Influence of the digital environment on literature for youth: Radical change in the handheld book. *Library Trends* 45 (4): 639-63.

_____. 1999. *Radical change: Books for youth in a digital age.* New York: H. W. Wilson.

Edmonds, Leslie et al. 1990. The effectiveness of an online catalog. *School Library Journal* 36 (10): 28-32.

Evans, Sara M., and Harry C. Boyte. 1986. *Free spaces: The sources of democratic change in America.* New York: Harper & Row.

Fasick, Adele. 1990. Research and measurement in library services to children. In *Evaluation strategies and techniques for public library children's services: A sourcebook*, edited by Jane Robbins. Madison: University of Wisconsin, School of Library and Information Studies.

Federal Interagency Forum on Child and Family Statistics. 1999. *America's children: Key national indicators of well-being.* Washington, D.C.: U.S. Government Printing Office.

Feinberg, Sandra, and Caryn Rogoff. 1998. Diversity takes children to a friendly family place. *American Libraries* 29 (7): 50-52.

Feinberg, Sandra, Joan F. Kuchner, and Sari Feldman. 1998. *Learning environments for young children: Rethinking library spaces and services.* Chicago: American Library Association.

Fenwick, Sara Innis. 1976. Library service to children and young people. *Library Trends* 25 (1): 329-60.

Filtering Facts. 1999. Friday letter, 29 October. <www.filteringfacts.org/> Last accessed 3 November 1999.

Fiore, Carole D. 1998. The numbers game: How to fatten your budget by using statistics. *School Library Journal* 44 (3): 104-6.

Fletcher, William I. 1876. Public libraries and the young. In *Public libraries in the United States: Their history, condition and management.* Washington, D.C.: Department of the Interior, Bureau of Education.

Fritz, Mark, and Greg Krikorian. 1998. Most states have already stiffened sentences on youths. *Los Angeles Times*, 27 March, A16.

Fuzesi, Stephen. 1999. Child-rearing by grandparents on the rise, census bureau says. *Los Angeles Times*, 1 July, A11.

Gag, Wanda. 1928. *Millions of cats.* New York: Coward-McCann.

Gantos, Jack. 1998. *Joey Pigza swallowed the key.* New York: Farrar, Straus and Giroux.

Garbarino, James, Nancy Dubrow, Kathleen Kostelny, and Carole Pardo. 1992. *Children in danger: Coping with the consequences of community violence.* San Francisco: Jossey-Bass.

Genco, Barbara A., Eleanor K. MacDonald, and Betsy Hearne. 1991. Juggling popularity and quality. *School Library Journal* 37 (3): 115-19.

George, Jean Craighead. 1972. *Julie of the wolves.* New York: HarperCollins.

Gladwell, Malcolm. 2000. *The tipping point: How little things can make a big difference.* Boston, Mass.: Little, Brown.

Goff, Lisa. 1999. Don't miss the bus! *American Demographics* 21 (8): 48-54.

Goldman, John J. 1998. Teacher accused of racial insensitivity is reinstated. *Los Angeles Times*, 26 November, A41.

Gregory, Vicki L., and Kathleen de la Peña McCook. 1998. Breaking the $30k barrier. *Library Journal* 123 (17): 32-38.

Griffin, Peg, and M. Susan Burns, eds. 1998. *Preventing reading difficulties in young children.* Washington, D.C.: National Academy Press.

Gross, Melissa. 1998. *Imposed queries in the school library media center: A descriptive study.* Ph.D. diss., University of California, Los Angeles. Abstract in *Dissertation Abstracts International* 59: 3261.

Hall, Richard B. 1999. Referenda resistance. *Library Journal* 124 (11): 48-51.

Halperin, Wendy Anderson. 1998. *Once upon a company: A true story.* New York: Orchard.

Hamilton, Virginia. 1999. Sentinels in long still rows. *American Libraries* 30 (6): 68-71.

Hawes, Joseph M. 1991. *The children's rights movement: A history of advocacy and protection.* Boston: Twayne.

Healy, Jane M. 1998. *Failure to connect: How computers affect our children's minds—for better and worse.* New York: Simon & Schuster.

Healy, Melissa. 1998. All work, less play is the burden of kids today. *Los Angeles Times*, 9 November, A19 and A20.

Hearne, Betsy, and Christine Jenkins. 1999. Sacred texts: What our foremothers left us in the way of psalms, proverbs, precepts, and practices. *Horn Book* 75 (5): 536-58.

Herron, Carolivia. 1997. *Nappy hair.* New York: Random House.

Heyns, Barbara. 1978. *Summer learning and the effects of schooling.* New York: Academic Press.

Hildebrand, Janet. 1997. Is privacy reserved for adults? Children's rights at the public library. In *School Library Journal's best: A reader for children's, young adult, and school librarians*, edited by Lillian N. Gerhardt. New York: Neal-Schuman. Originally published in *School Library Journal* 37 (January 1991).

Himmel, Ethel, and William James Wilson. 1998. *Planning for results: A public library transformation process.* Chicago: American Library Association.

Hirsh, Sandra G. 1997. How do children find information on different types of tasks? Children's use of the Science Library Catalog. *Library Trends* 45 (4): 725-45.

Hoban, Tana. 1993. *Black on white.* New York: Greenwillow.

Holt, Glen E., and Donald Elliott. 1998. Proving your library's worth: A test case. *Library Journal* 123 (18): 42-44.

Holt, Glen E., and Leslie Edmonds Holt. 1999. What's it worth? *School Library Journal* 45 (6): 47.

Holt, Glen E., Donald Elliott, and Amonia Moore. 1999. Placing a value on public library services. *Public Libraries* 38 (2): 98-108.

Houlgate, Laurence D. 1980. *The child and the state: A normative theory of juvenile rights.* Baltimore: Md.: Johns Hopkins University Press.

An interview with Brenda Laurel. 1998. In *From Barbie to Mortal Kombat: Gender and computer games,* edited by Justine Cassell and Henry Jenkins. Cambridge, Mass.: MIT Press.

Jacobson, Frances. 1998. Personal communication with the author. Los Angeles, 18 June.

Jeffery, Debby Ann. 1995. *Literate beginnings: Programs for babies and toddlers.* Chicago: American Library Association.

Jenkins, Christine A. 1994. Children's services, public. In *Encyclopedia of library history*, edited by Wayne A. Wiegand and Donald G. Davis Jr. New York: Garland.

_____. 1996. Women of ALA youth services and professional jurisdiction: Of nightingales, Newberies, realism, and the right books, 1937-1945. *Library Trends* 44 (4): 813-39.

Johnson, George. 1999. It's a fact: Faith and theory collide over evolution. *New York Times*, 15 August, D1 and D4.

Judge halts vouchers at Ohio schools. 1999. *Los Angeles Times*, 25 August, A15.

Kafai, Yasmin. 1993. *Minds in play: Computer game design as a context for children's learning.* Hillsdale, N.J.: Erlbaum.

Kantrowitz, Barbara, and Pat Wingert. 1998. Learning at home: Does it pass the test? *Newsweek*, 5 October, 64-70.

_____. 1999. The truth about teens. *Newsweek*, 18 October, 62-72.

Kassin, Michael. 1999. Tall Tree: Counting the leaves. *Public Libraries* 38 (2): 120-23.

Katz, Jon. 1996. The rights of kids in the digital age. *Wired* 4 (7): 120-23, 166-70.

Keats, Ezra Jack. 1964. *Whistle for Willie.* New York: Viking.

Kemp, Roger L. 1999. A city manager looks at trends affecting public libraries. *Public Libraries* 38 (2): 116-19.

Kids need libraries: School and public libraries preparing the youth of today for the world of tomorrow. 1997. In *School Library Journal's best: A reader for children's, young adult, and school librarians*, edited by Lillian N. Gerhardt. New York: Neal-Schuman. Originally published in *School Library Journal* 36 (April 1990).

Kohn, Alfie. 1992. *No contest: The case against competition.* Boston: Houghton Mifflin.

_____. 1993. *Punished by rewards: The trouble with gold stars, incentive plans, A's, praise, and other bribes.* Boston: Houghton Mifflin.

Kuklin, Susan. 1998. *Iqbal Masih and the crusaders against child slavery.* New York: Holt.

Ladd, Rosalind Ekman, ed. 1996. *Children's rights re-visioned: Philosophical readings.* Belmont, Calif.: Wadsworth.

La Ganga, Maria L. 1998. Bilingual ed initiative wins easily. *Los Angeles Times*, 3 June, A1 and A24.

Larrick, Nancy. 1965. The all-white world of children's books. *Saturday Review*, 11 September, 63-65.

Leapman, Michael. 1998. *Witnesses to war: Eight true-life stories of Nazi persecution.* New York: Viking.

Let boy read, orders mayor. 1999. *American Libraries* 30 (6): 41-42.

Libraries and the Internet toolkit. 2000. Chicago: American Library Association.

Lisle, Janet Taylor. 1989. *Afternoon of the elves.* New York: Orchard.

Locke, Jill. 1992. Summer reading activities—way back when. *Journal of Youth Services in Libraries* 6 (1): 72-77.

Lowry, Lois. 1993. *The giver.* Boston: Houghton Mifflin.

Lundin, Anne. 1996. The pedagogical context of women in children's services and literature scholarship. *Library Trends* 44 (4): 840-50.

_____. 1998. Anne Carroll Moore (1871-1961): "I have spun out a long thread." In *Reclaiming the American library past: Writing the women in*, edited by Suzanne Hildenbrand. Norwood, N.J.: Ablex.

Machado, Julie et al. 2000. A survey of best practices in youth services around the country. *Journal of Youth Services in Libraries* 13 (2): 30-35.

Madden, Susan B. 1997. Learning at home. In *School Library Journal's best: A reader for children's, young adult, and school librarians*, edited by Lillian N. Gerhardt. New York: Neal-Schuman. Originally published in *School Library Journal* 37 (July 1991).

Manley, Will. 1990. Crisis and opportunity: A call for quality. *Wilson Library Bulletin* 65 (3): 63-65.

Marchionini, Gary, and Herman Maurer. 1995. The role of digital libraries in teaching and learning. *Communications of the ACM* 38 (4): 67-75.

Margolis, Rick. Native American fact—or fiction? 1999. *School Library Journal* 45 (6): 16.

Markey, Penny. 1999. Report: Library latchkey survey, June 1-June 7, 1999. County of Los Angeles Public Library.

Martin, Bill. 1992. *Brown bear, brown bear, what do you see?* New York: Holt.

McClure, Charles R. et al. 1987. *Planning and role setting for public libraries.* Chicago: American Library Association.

McElderry, Margaret K. 1997. Remarkable women: Anne Carroll Moore & Company. In *School Library Journal's best: A reader for children's, young adult, and school librarians*, edited by Lillian N. Gerhardt. New York: Neal-Schuman.

McLaughlin, Milbrey W., Merita A. Irby, and Juliet Langman. 1994. *Urban sanctuaries: Neighborhood organizations in the lives and futures of inner-city youth.* San Francisco: Jossey-Bass.

Mediavilla, Cindy. 1998. Homework assistance programs in public libraries: Helping Johnny read. In *Young adults and public libraries: A handbook of materials and services*, edited by Mary Anne Nichols and C. Allen Nichols. Westport, Conn.: Greenwood.

_____. 1999. Personal communication with the author. Los Angeles, 3 March.

Metoyer-Duran, Cheryl. 1993. *Gatekeepers in ethnolinguistic communities.* Norwood, N.J.: Ablex.

Minkel, Walter, and Roxanne Hsu Feldman. 1999. *Delivering Web reference services to young people.* Chicago: American Library Association.

Minow, Martha. 1996. Rights for the next generation: A feminist approach to children's rights. In *Children's rights re-visioned: Philosophical readings*, edited by Rosalind Ekman Ladd. Belmont, Calif.: Wadsworth.

Molz, Redmond Kathleen, and Phyllis Dain. 1999. *Civic space/cyberspace: The American public library in the information age.* Cambridge, Mass.: MIT Press.

Mondowney, JoAnn G. 1997. Licensed to learn: Drivers' training for the Internet. *School Library Journal* 42 (1): 32-34.

Monmaney, Terence, and Greg Krikorian. 1998. Violent culture, media share blame, experts say. *Los Angeles Times*, 26 March, A16 and A17.

Moore, Anne Carroll. 1969. *My roads to childhood: Views and reviews of children's books.* Boston: Horn Book.

Moore, E. 1961. Serving students in time of crisis. *California Librarian* 22: 219-24.

Morse, Suzanne W. 1998. Five building blocks for successful communities. In *The Community of the future*, edited by Frances Hesselbein. San Francisco: Jossey-Bass.

Murnane, Richard J., and Frank Levy. 1996. *Teaching the new basic skills: Principles for educating children to thrive in a changing economy.* New York: Free Press.

Murphy, Kim. 1998. Seattle's school program sets off marketing frenzy. *Los Angeles Times*, 9 April, A1 and A14.

National leadership grants. 1998. Institute of Museum and Library Services. <www.imls.fed.us/nlg98list.htm> Last accessed 14 July 1999.

National Research Council. 1998. *Preventing reading difficulties in children,* edited by Catherine E. Snow, Susan M. Burns, and Peg Griffin. Washington, D.C.: National Academy Press.

_____. 1999. *Starting out right: A guide to promoting children's reading success,* edited by Susan M. Burns, Peg Griffin, and Catherine E. Snow. Washington, D.C.: National Academy Press.

Native American fact—or fiction? 1999. *School Library Journal* 45 (6): 16.

Negroponte, Nicholas. 1995. *Being digital.* New York: Knopf.

Nespecca, Sue McCleaf. 1994. *Library programming for families with young children.* New York: Neal-Schuman.

Norton, Mary. 1953. *The borrowers.* San Diego, Calif.: Harcourt Brace.

O'Connor, Anne-Marie. 1999. Ranks of homeless children on the rise, study finds. *Los Angeles Times*, 1 July, B1 and B10.

Olcott, Frances Jenkins. 1905. Rational library work with children and the preparation for it. In *Proceedings of the American Library Association Conference,* 71-75. Chicago: American Library Association.

Olson, Renee. 1999. Whither the librarians? *School Library Journal* 45 (6): 14.

Orlev, Uri. 1984. *The island on bird street.* Boston: Houghton Mifflin.

Osborne, David, and Ted Gaebler. 1992. *Reinventing government: How the entrepreneurial spirit is transforming the public sector.* Reading, Mass.: Addison-Wesley.

Papert, Seymour. 1993. *The children's machine: Rethinking school in the age of the computer.* New York: Basic Books.

_____. 1996. *The connected family: Bridging the digital generation gap.* Atlanta: Longstreet Press.

Pasadena Public Library. 1999. Summer reading club. <www.ci.pasadena. ca.us/librarykids/summer.html> Last accessed 12 August 1999.

Paterson, Katherine. 1998. *Still summoned by books.* Los Angeles: UCLA Department of Library and Information Science.

Paulsen, Gary. 1987. *Hatchet.* New York: Bradbury.

Perlmutter, Jane. 1999. Which online resources are right for your collection? *School Library Journal* 45 (6): 27-29.

Peterson, Paul E., and Chad Noyes. 1998. School choice in Milwaukee. In *New schools for a new century: The redesign of urban education,* edited by Diane Ravitch and Joseph P. Viteritti. New Haven, Conn.: Yale University Press.

Powell, Colin. 1998. I wasn't left to myself. *Newsweek,* 27 April, 32.

Public Library Data Service. 1997. *Statistical report '97.* Chicago: Public Library Association.

_____. 1998. *Statistical report '98.* Chicago: Public Library Association.

The Pura Belpre award. American Library Association. <www.ala.org/alsc/ belpre.html> Last accessed 20 July 1999.

Purple Moon ships highly anticipated CD-ROM friendship adventures for girls. 1997. Press release. Purple Moon.

Py-Lieberman, Beth. 1999. The colors of childhood. *Smithsonian* 30 (8): 32-36.

Ravitch, Diane, and Joseph P. Viteritti. 1997. Introduction to *New schools for a new century: The redesign of urban education,* edited by Diane Ravitch and Joseph P. Viteritti. New Haven, Conn.: Yale University Press.

ReadQuest. 1999. Multnomah County Public Library. <www.multnomah.lib. or.us/lib/summer/menu.html> Last accessed 8 July 1999.

Read to me L.A. (n.d.) Fact sheet. Los Angeles Public Library.

Reagan, Robert. 1997. Homework centers: Four important pluses. *Public Libraries* 36 (1): 20-21.

Rheingold, Howard. 1993. *The virtual community: Homesteading on the electronic frontier.* Reading, Mass.: Addison-Wesley.

Riechel, Rosemarie. 1991. *Reference services for children and young adults.* Hamden, Conn.: Library Professional Publications.

Rinaldi, Ann. 1999. *My heart is on the ground: The diary of Nannie Little Rose, a Sioux girl.* New York: Scholastic.

Rockfield, Gary. 1998. Beyond library power: Reader's Digest adds public libraries to the mix. *School Library Journal* 44 (1): 30-33.

Rollock, Barbara. 1988. *Public library services for children.* Hamden, Conn.: Library Professional Publications.

Rong, Xue Lan, and Judith Preissle. 1998. *Educating immigrant students: What we need to know to meet the challenges.* Thousand Oaks, Calif.: Corwin/Sage.

Rowling, J. K. 1998. *Harry Potter and the sorcerer's stone.* New York: Scholastic.

Rushkoff, Douglas. 1996. *Playing the future: How kids' culture can teach us to thrive in an age of chaos.* New York: HarperCollins.

Sager, Donald. 1997. Beating the homework blues. *Public Libraries* 36 (1): 19-23.

Sahagun, Louis. 1998. In any language, the fight is on over bilingual instruction. *Los Angeles Times*, 16 April, A5.

Sanders, Rickie, and Mattson, Mark T. 1998. *Growing up in America: An atlas of youth in the USA.* New York: Simon & Schuster/Macmillan.

Sandvig, Christian. 1998. Report of findings: Nonparticipant observation and interviews, San Francisco electronic library project. San Francisco Public Library. <206.14.7.53/nsf/evaledc.html> Last accessed 22 July 1993.

San Francisco Public Library. 1999a. Electronic library project. <206.14.7.53/nsf> Last accessed 22 July 1999.

_____. Office of Children's and Youth Services. 1999b. Selection criteria for educational software. <206.14.7.53/nsf/softwarecriteria.html> Last accessed 22 July 1999.

_____. 1999c. Selection criteria for web pages. <206.14.7.53/nsf/www criteria.html> Last accessed 22 July, 1999.

Sashkin, Marshall, and Kenneth J. Kiser. 1993. *Putting total quality management to work.* San Francisco: Barrett-Koehler.

Sayers, Frances Clarke. 1965. Lose not the nightingale. In *Summoned by books,* compiled by Marjeanne Jensen Blinn. New York: Viking.

_____. 1965. Writing for children: A responsibility and an art. In *Summoned by books.* New York: Viking.

_____. 1972. *Anne Carroll Moore.* New York: Atheneum.

Scheps, Susan G. 1999. Homeschoolers in the library. *School Library Journal* 45 (2): 38-39.

Schmidt, Warren H., and Jerome P. Finnigan. 1992. *The race without a finish line: America's quest for total quality.* San Francisco: Jossey-Bass.

Schon, Donald A. 1983. *The reflective practitioner: How professionals think in action.* New York: Basic Books.

Serious crime plagues 20% of U.S. schools. 1998. *Los Angeles Times*, 20 March, A19.

Shannon, David. 1998. *No, David!* New York: Scholastic/Blue Sky Press.

Shaughnessy, Thomas W. 1993. Benchmarking, total quality management, and libraries. *Library Administration and Management* 7: 7-12.

Shuit, Douglas P. 1998. 8th-graders break down barriers in cyberspace. *Los Angeles Times*, 1 January, B1 and B5.

Simon, Stephanie. 1999. Paying an adult price for crime. *Los Angeles Times*, 6 August, A1 and A13-14.

Sims, Rudine [Bishop]. 1982. *Shadow and substance: Afro-American experience in contemporary children's fiction.* Urbana, Ill.: National Council of Teachers of English.

Slapin, Beverly, and Doris Seale. 1992. *Through Indian eyes: The native experience in children's books.* Philadelphia: New Society.

Somerville, Mary. 1998. Facing the shortage of children's librarians: Updating the challenge. *American Libraries* 29 (9): 50-54.

Sommerville, John. 1982. *The rise and fall of childhood.* Beverly Hills, Calif.: Sage.

Spinelli, Jerry. 1990. *Maniac Magee.* Boston: Little, Brown.

Staerkel, Kathleen, Mary Fellows, and Sue McCleaf Nespecca. 1995. *Youth services librarians as managers: A how-to guide from budgeting to personnel.* Chicago: American Library Association/Association for Library Service to Children.

Subrahmanyam, Kaveri, and Patricia M. Greenfield. 1998. Computer games for girls: What makes them play? In *From Barbie to Mortal Kombat: Gender and computer games*, edited by Justine Cassell and Henry Jenkins. Cambridge, Mass.: MIT Press.

Symons, Ann K. 1997. Sizing up sites: How to judge what you find on the web. *School Library Journal* 43 (4): 22-25.

Tapscott, Don. 1998. *Growing up digital: The rise of the net generation.* New York: McGraw-Hill.

Taylor, Kimberly Hayes. 1999. Twin cities districts face language, cultural barriers. *Minneapolis Star Tribune*, 20 September, A1 and A8.

Teale, William H. 1995. Public libraries and emergent literacy: Helping set the foundation for school success. In *Achieving school readiness: Public libraries and national education goal no. 1*, edited by Barbara Froling Immroth and Viki Ash-Geisler. Chicago: American Library Association.

Thomas, Fannette H. 1990. Early appearances of children's reading rooms in public libraries. *Journal of Youth Services* 4: 81-85.

Thomas, Jo. 1998. Digitized artifacts are making knowledge available to all, on line. *New York Times*, 19 November, A21.

Turkle, Sherry. 1995. *Life on the screen: Identity in the age of the Internet.* New York: Simon & Schuster.

Tyack, David, and Larry Cuban. 1995. *Tinkering toward Utopia: A century of public school reform.* Cambridge, Mass.: Harvard University Press.

Uchitelle, Louis. 1999. The American middle, just getting by. *New York Times*, 1 August, C1 and C13.

U.S. Census Bureau. 1993. *We the American children.* Washington, D.C.: U.S. Department of Commerce, Census Bureau.

U. S. Department of Education, National Center for Education Statistics. 1995. *Services and resources for children and young adults in public libraries.* Washington, D.C.: U.S. Department of Education.

Vail, Kathleen. 1997. Girlware: Software companies are targeting girls, but is their marketing on the mark? *Electronic School,* June 1997. Cover story. <www.electronicschool.com/0697f1.html> Last accessed 3 November 1999.

Vandergrift, Kay. 1996. Female advocacy and harmonious voices: A history of public library services and publishing for children in the United States. *Library Trends* 44 (4): 683-718.

Van House, Nancy et al. 1987. *Output measures for public libraries: A manual of standardized procedures.* 2d ed. Chicago: American Library Association.

Viti, Thomas. 1997. The role of the public library in homework assistance. *Public Libraries* 36 (1): 21-22.

Volume of children's work in the United States. 1913. *Bulletin of the American Library Association* 7 (4): 287-90.

Walter, Virginia A. 1992. *Output measures for public library service to children: A manual of standardized procedures.* Chicago: American Library Association.

_____. 1994. The information needs of children. *Advances in Librarianship* 40:111-29.

_____. 1995. *Output measures and more: Planning and evaluating young adult services in public libraries.* Chicago: American Library Association.

_____. 1997a. Becoming digital: Policy implications for library youth services. *Library Trends* 45 (4): 585-601.

_____. 1997b. Starting early: Multimedia for the tricycle set. *Book Links* 6 (5): 26-33.

Walter, Virginia A., and Penny Markey. 1997. Parent perceptions of a summer reading program. *Journal of Youth Services* 11: 49-65.

Walter, Virginia A. et al. 1996. The science library catalog: A springboard for information literacy. *School Library Media Quarterly* 24 (2): 105-10.

Watson, Dana. 1998. Multicultural children's literature selection and evaluation: Incorporating the World Wide Web. *The Acquisitions Librarian* 20:171-83.

Willett, Holly G. 1995. *Public library youth services: A public policy approach.* Norwood, N.J.: Ablex.

Wilson, Pauline. 1997. Children's services in a time of change. In *School Library Journal's best: A reader for children's, young adult, and school librarians*, edited by Lillian N. Gerhardt. New York: Neal-Schuman. Originally published in *School Library Journal* 25 (February 1979).

Winerip, Michael. 1998. Schools for sale. *New York Times Magazine*, 14 June, 42-48, 80, 86-89.

Winton, Richard. 1999. Libraries struggle in role as child care providers. *Los Angeles Times*, 10 February, A1, A24, and A25.

Wishy, Bernard. 1968. *The child and the republic: The dawn of modern American child nurture.* Philadelphia: University of Pennsylvania Press.

Wohlstetter, Priscilla, Susan Albers Mohrman, and Peter J. Robertson. 1997. Successful school-based management: A lesson for restructuring urban schools. In *New schools for a new century: The redesign of urban education*, edited by Diane Ravitch and Joseph P. Viteritti. New Haven, Conn.: Yale University Press.

Wolf, Bernard. 1997. *HIV positive.* New York: Dutton.

Yep, Laurence. 1975. *Dragonwings.* New York: HarperCollins.

Index

Virginia A. Walter has an M.L.S. from the University of California, Berkeley, and a Ph.D. in Public Administration from the University of Southern California. She worked for more than twenty years in public libraries, most recently as Children's Services Coordinator for Los Angeles Public Library. She is now an associate professor in UCLA's Department of Information Studies.

Her earlier publications are *Output Measures for Public Library Service to Children* and *Output Measures and More: Planning and Evaluating Young Adult Services in Pubic Libraries,* both published by ALA. In 1999-2000, she served as the president of the Association for Library Service to Children, a division of the American Library Association.